Belted Galloway cattle survey the surrounds of Allen and Lizette Snaith's Victorian property, Warialda.

country homes

Trail riding horses graze among the snow gums at Dinner Plain in Victoria's High Country.

COUNTRY STYLE

country homes IN AUSTRALIA

30 YEARS OF LIFE ON THE LAND

contents

1989 TO 2000

RURAL AUSTRALIA HADN'T been in a rush to embrace sophistication. Towards the end of the 20th century however, early imposing buildings in regional towns were ready for restoration and priced accordingly. *Country Style* emerged to provide the guidance and, for many, the motivation to link Country and Style.

While planning the first issue of the magazine, the editorial team realised that none of them had any country living experience. They swooped on me because I was dividing my time between the city and a property I'd bought in the Central West of NSW.

The name of the column, Country Squire, was created by founding editor Susan Hurley and in it I was to provide a lighthearted look at the misadventures of a tree-changer. Little could I have imagined that I'd still be writing the column 30 years later.

Heritage historian Ian Evans wrote: "Everyone who owns and cares for an old house and endeavours to retain its original character, is doing their bit to preserve our heritage."

Commendable, yes, but *Country Style* was also a champion of the creative and charming. As well as restored flour mills near Launceston, we beckoned our readers to a brave new world of bachelor and spinster balls, one-teacher schools, tapestry, growing and preserving dill pickled cucumbers, bentwood chairs, needlework samplers, and golden corn cakes with bacon.

Kingsley Amis once wrote that he had never understood why anyone agreed to go on being rustic after about 1400. *Country Style* told him why.
Words by Country Squire, Rob Ingram

Country Style emerged to offer guidance for those seeking a quality lifestyle away from metropolitan madness.

Top: A favourite corner of the garden. Above: The real ducks were camera shy – these papier-mâché fowl were made by Ruth's daughter Helen. Below: Gums and palm trees tower above a rockery of shrubs and groundcovers.
they had been used in a flood to rescue the sheep."
Ruth was widowed only a few years after her marriage. She continued to run the property, raise three young children, cope with bushfires and floods and still find time for her expanding garden. She felt she was carrying on her husband's wishes as well as her own in making it a place of beauty and tranquillity.
The house was built around 1876 and features an unusual double bullnose roofline and wide verandah typical of early Australian architecture. Timber for the pineboard walls was cut on the property. The cedar front doors have pretty etched glass. A wide entrance contains a cedar arch and branches off into
The front verandah with a close-up of the flounced roofline – one of the most
TO HAVE AND TO HOLD
AUSTRALIAN
COUNTRY STYLE
Paradise Found
A Romantic, Drought-Defying Garden
A Church Converted
Cottage Living 1920s Style
Napery for the Best Tables
Woolly Knits and Weaves
The Freshest Country Kitchens
AUSTRALIAN
COUNTRY STYLE
Winter's Tales
Stories to Warm the Heart
Historic Homes
Country Living
Creative Lives
Rugging up:
Romantic Weekends Away
Delicious Savoury Pies
Escaping to the Sunshine Coast
MAGAZINE OF THE YEAR
HANGING PLACES
High Country
Calling
distant lands
ns embodies all its namesake represents — the sun, healthy crops
osperity — and peace in a faraway place for a pair of wanderers.
By Carol Twopeny. Photography by Don Brice
AUSTRALIAN
COUNTRY STYLE
HOME TIME
Castles and Cottages, Tea Tales, Winter Escapes, Woolly Jumpers in the Wild, A Wok in the Kitchen
VISIT A COUNTRY COOKING SCHOOL
VICTORIA'S GREAT OCEAN ROAD

LOOKING BACK AT 30 YEARS

2001

TO

2010

IT WOULD BE fair to say that *Country Style* rolled into the Noughties and its second decade firmly on a mission to bring the beauty, diversity and resilience of modern Australian country life to our readership. The magazine had a couple of facelifts while still travelling to remote and regional areas bringing back our regular heartland stories of beautiful homes, gardens and inspiring people and stunning places.

When our relaunch issue of March 2008 arrived, readers who had collected every single copy of *Country Style* were not all delighted by the change in colour on the magazine's spine — their pristine white stacks were now every colour of the rainbow!

But also in this decade, we visited several communities struck by natural disasters. Among them was in the aftermath of the bushfires that burnt through the Grampians National Park and surrounding farmland in Victoria in 2006, and again in the wake of the Black Saturday fires in 2009 which swept through vast swathes of Victoria creating almost unprecedented destruction. We were struck by the unbreakable spirit of rural communities and the can-do attitude and generosity of friends, neighbours, volunteers and complete strangers.

It was then that we met Kevin and Rhonda Butler, who had just founded the now renowned national volunteer-based disaster relief program, BlazeAid, after their own farmland was burnt. Then, almost just to show us what a fickle climate we live in, by November that year we were in northern NSW reporting on massive floods.
Words by Virginia Imhoff

The magazine underwent a few makeovers during the decade from 2001 to 2010.

LOOKING BACK AT 30 YEARS

2011 TO NOW

AND SO NOW *Country Style* is 30 and all grown up. And something's going on in the country. There's a new energy out there in the regions. This decade has firmly entrenched the words 'tree-changer' and 'sustainability' into the lexicon.

As property prices drive people away from the city, more of us are finding country towns and regions offer a better lifestyle alternative. We meet parents wanting to bring up their children in small communities, with fresh air and freedom. Others ditching city-based careers to get their hands in the soil and grow organic produce or flowers, or ethically raise livestock. Some finding new income streams by sharing their knowledge and creativity with others in workshops and events. Bartering and sharing produce are the 'new black'.

We feature the chefs who design menus around produce that comes out of their restaurant garden each day, or lands on the doorstep from the farmer down the road. We started the schools' Harvest Table competition to discover what kids are learning about growing and preparing fresh, seasonal food in school kitchen garden programs. Meeting our Harvest Table finalists in their kitchen garden classroom is always a highlight for the team at *Country Style,* and always a delicious treat. And we love finding the new creative businesses that are being launched online from remote areas, servicing others in remote regions and beyond.

After 30 years of showcasing the country, we have learnt that the more things change in the country, the more they stay the same.

Words by Virginia Imhoff

gaucho club
new vintage
TRADITION IS MIXING WITH INNOVATION IN THE RUTHERGLEN WINE REGION.
HOME AGAIN
ONCE FALLING INTO DISREPAIR, A COLONIAL HOMESTEAD NOW OFFERS VISITORS A PEACEFUL RETREAT.
BUCKLAND TASMANIA
COUNTRY STYLE
ESCAPE THE EVERYDAY
island of dreams
WIN $5000 Enter our short story competition
HOLIDAY READING SPECIAL
dream world
people | POOWONG EAST
'Tree-changer' and 'sustainability' have become the buzzwords of the past decade, which has seen people moving to the country as they re-evaluate their lives.
time to flower
COUNTRY STYLE
ESCAPE THE EVERYDAY
life on the land
AUSTRALIA'S UNBREAKABLE SPIRIT
LIVING ON AN OUTBACK STATION IN THE DROUGHT
THE CALL OF HOME A couple's return to the family property

Cattle graze near Coolabunia, just over 200 kilometres north-west of Brisbane in Queensland's South Burnett Region.

On display at Deb Kavaliunas' seaside cottage is a carefully laid out collection of eggs bought from a farmer who gathered them in the 1950s. **FACING PAGE** A "Zen-inspired" watercolour painted by Deb, at far left, mixes with nostalgic pieces in her dining room.

HOME

DEB KAVALIUNAS

QUEENSCLIFF VICTORIA

"IT TOOK ON A LIFE OF ITS OWN AND, LIKE THE OTHER ROOMS, TURNED OUT MORE LIKE A MUSEUM."

"**I WAS BORN** a collector and simply can't remember a time when I didn't gather things that caught my eye," remarks Deb Kavaliunas as she looks around her seaside cottage in Queenscliff, on Victoria's Bellarine Peninsula. Brimming with exquisitely assembled collections, almost every surface displays groupings: birds' nests, feathers and cages; books, bottles and antique toys; coral, shells and other sea treasures.

Queenscliff has been Deb's home for a little more than 12 months, though she has spent nearly 30 years living in nearby towns on the Bellarine. "People here are very friendly and life here just seems to be less hectic than in surrounding towns," she says.

Tucked away in a quiet side street, Deb's home is a cottage built in 1836 for a blacksmith. Its facade is painted a chalky sea blue, and although the years have seen many of its period features stripped away, the home retains the traditional cottage layout of four front formal rooms and bedrooms, with a kitchen and a series of add-on rooms at the rear.

Deb's foraging has produced the home's most striking feature — those wonderful collections. Inside, display cabinets exhibit her assemblages, some with quite eclectic combinations: doll's house furniture nestled with antique apothecary bottles, or a boat propeller beside a butterfly collection. Mismatched, perhaps, but thanks to Deb's creative eye it all works.

"I suppose I've come to think of my style as being like that of a museum, and the one constant element has always been the search for natural character — things that shine on their own merit, not because there is a brand name on it," she says. "The most special things are the ones that carry the weight of common history, everyday lives of everyday folk. Unfortunately, they're highly covetable now, so they're harder to find."

The study, which Deb says is her favourite room, was originally intended to be a studio in which to create her assemblages. "It took on a life of its own and, like the other rooms, turned out more like a museum," she says with a smile.

The rear verandah and garden are also full of finds. Old furniture and building materials such as wooden mantels and finials, chandeliers and even sea eagles' nests are propped, seemingly haphazardly, around the yard.

Deb's passion for collecting quite naturally led to a career as a second-hand dealer. "I had stalls at the Mill Markets in Geelong and Newcomb for eight years and loved it because it allowed me to forage and to put things together," she says. "Although it did amuse me how miffed I felt when a significant piece sold and ruined my display!"

Her venture, Shed Off Pako, is run with like-minded collectors Adrian and Thea Brown near Geelong's antiques strip, Pakington Street.

When she isn't travelling the countryside looking for more treasures, Deb is revelling in her new role as grandmother to William, now seven months old.

"He doesn't know it yet, but he already has an amazing collection of vintage toys, including a very special antique wooden boat!" she confides.

Deb's approach to creating a home is all about knowing what works best for yourself. "You learn to trust yourself. Not long ago this way of living and collecting was kind of frowned on — nobody wanted this stuff," she says. "But I persisted because it felt right, and now it all naturally connects as if it was collected in one go. Your own way of seeing the world will always work best."

Originally published in Country Style, August 2012.

A still life by local artist Ryan Brearley in the kitchen.

CLOCKWISE, FROM TOP LEFT Deb Kavaliunas with Phil, her Shetland sheepdog; apothecary bottles, plaster building vents and doll's house furniture; the 1836 blacksmith's cottage that's now Deb's home; an eclectic display of butterfly collections, an oil painting and a boat's propeller. **FACING PAGE** Fascinating objects are displayed on almost every surface.

Vintage fabric airing in the back garden. **FACING PAGE, CLOCKWISE, FROM TOP LEFT** In Deb's study, a cabinet of curiosities — nests collected out of breeding season by Deb over 20 years, sea treasures bought years ago from dealers, antique books and a vintage camera; antique mannequins and faded floral artworks in the bedroom of Deb Kavaliunas; artfully arranged second-hand wares await shipment to Deb's shop; a sea eagle's nest propped above more collections on the back porch.

Lisa and Glen Rundell watch six-year-old son Tom get hands-on in the workshop. **FACING PAGE** A 'Continuous Arm' Windsor chair that was crafted by a student.

PEOPLE

GLEN RUNDELL

ARTISAN WOODWORKER

A RARE BREED of artisan, Glen Rundell is a woodworker from Kyneton, in Victoria, who makes traditional Windsor chairs. This classic sculptural piece of furniture is, in his eyes, "nothing short of perfection" in craftsmanship. "I love it for its tradition and engineering, and the fact that it's all made with hand tools," he says. "The seat is carved and there are no nails, no screws, only good woodworking techniques."

Glen was so keen to learn these skills that in 2009 he decided to travel to the United States to study with a master craftsman. "No-one was making Windsor chairs in Australia at the time," he says. "I had always made things out of wood, but I wanted to go to America with a view to doing something with the knowledge I brought back. So I sold my motorbike and bought a ticket to the United States to learn how to make them from Curtis Buchanan, in Tennessee."

Dating back nearly 300 years, the Windsor chair style was first made in England in the Buckinghamshire forests. The makers took their chairs to Windsor (hence the name) where they were shipped down the Thames to London. When the style reached America, it was further refined. "The Americans pared down the final details and accentuated everything, and I think they did it better than the English," Glen says.

Both Glen and his wife Lisa are passionate about reviving traditional manual skills. Lisa expresses her love of craft in leatherwork, making leather bags she lines with a beautiful fabric, attaching handles of English bridle leather. She also makes satchels and small rectangular bags copied from a vintage German lunch box. All are traditionally copper riveted and have a soft waxed finish. Self-taught, she explains, "I've always loved leather but could never find a bag I liked, so I made one and a lot of people wanted to buy it."

The couple have lifelong interests in all kinds of crafts, although early in their working lives Glen trained as a plumber and Lisa went into marketing and advertising. "I grew up on a farm in Victoria's High Country," Glen says. "My grandfather was a carpenter and owned a saddlery shop in later years, and I hand-stitched leather belts for fun — leatherwork has been in my family for a long time. When Lisa and I met in 1996, she was making wedding jewellery — she can turn her hand to anything."

In 2011, they took a deep breath, packed up their suburban home and with their young son, Tom, now six, moved to Kyneton, an hour north of Melbourne. The plan was to concentrate on what had been, until then, their hobbies. "Glen's trip to America was life-changing for us," Lisa says. "We wanted to explore traditional crafts and to have a go, and the city wasn't the right place. This town was vibrant and not too far from Melbourne, so we rented for eight months until this interesting old building came on the market."

The lovely old weatherboard store on Kyneton's Piper Street now bears the name Rundell & Rundell and is a showcase for Lisa's bags and Glen's chairs. The family lives behind the store, which is also a gallery for an extraordinary collection of traditional handmade items from around the country and overseas. The pair has formed Lost Trades Australia, an initiative to promote and preserve manual skills and traditional trades, and they recently held the first Lost Trades Fair in Kyneton, which attracted 7000 visitors to the town.

In a side street, Glen has a workshop, where he also holds classes in chair-making. Opening the door, there's the sudden waft of freshly worked timber from students' chairs in various stages of completion. Glen says they're all future heirlooms that will last for generations, including a nearly completed 'Continuous Arm' Windsor chair that is the work of a 19-year-old. The 'Rocker' version is also popular with the students, as well as three-legged stools with smooth curvaceous seats called perches.

Glen likes to use English elm and pin oak for the seat, both of which he looks to salvage from around the district. It can take anywhere from three to 80 days to make a chair, he says, "depending on how complex it is". The finished chair is then painted with up to five layers of milk paint. Offcuts are used to make simple Shaker-style boxes, sold in the store.

The Shaker ethos, developed by a Protestant sect in America during the 18th and 19th centuries, also appeals to Glen. "They were incredibly frugal, clever people and the things they made were well thought out, inventive, with quality workmanship," he says.

Lisa and Glen's hands are rarely still, yet 12 months ago they took on another labour of love — the last piece of the jigsaw to complete their new life in Kyneton. They bought a dilapidated 1860s farmhouse in a nearby town, just begging to be rescued. As luck would have it, the home couldn't have fallen into more competent hands.

"We were waiting for the perfect house," Lisa says. "And this is our project for the next 10 years."

Originally published in Country Style, May 2014.

CLOCKWISE, FROM TOP LEFT A selection of Shaker boxes and carriers; Glen uses a spokeshave to fashion a chair spindle; old harness makers, round knives and a glue pot; a 'Continuous Arm' chair and other carefully crafted wares in a corner of the shop.

In the heart of Victoria's Surf Coast hinterland, owners Fran Derham and Michael Robertson have created their modern take on a log cabin. **FACING PAGE** Handmade ceramics by Andrei Davidoff.

HOME

FRAN DERHAM AND MICHAEL ROBERTSON

WENSLEYDALE VICTORIA

THERE ARE MANY good reasons why Fran Derham and Michael Robertson feel so deeply connected to their farm in the lush hinterland of Victoria's Surf Coast. Without doubt, however, the most heartfelt of those harks back to 2013. "Michael proposed to me here, so the farm is very close to our hearts," Fran says. "It was pretty funny — he was taking me to an amazing spot at one of our dams that is set with really nice trees, but we only got halfway when the clouds opened up with torrential rain. We didn't quite make it, so he proposed on the cow track on a hillside in the pouring rain!"

Michael, 36, a builder, and Fran, 35, a television producer and co-owner of Melbourne-based production company Cos We Can, now have two children — Woody, two, and six-month-old daughter, Quinn. Their property is set on 32 hectares of rolling pasture that backs onto a forest on the western Victorian coast. "It's half an hour through state forest from Aireys Inlet on the coast, and 20 minutes from Birregurra, in a little pocket called Wensleydale," Fran says.

It was Michael who found the property in 2012, and then drove the dream to build the rustic timber-clad home. "Michael is the type of person who comes home and says, 'I've bought this!'" Fran says. "He grew up in Ballarat and always wanted to have a country property as a farm escape, and give his kids a similar experience. Michael was driving through one day and fell in love with the area. He was inspired by the classic Australian shed and always envisioned a really simple all-wooden shack here."

Fran also loved the region. She grew up in Melbourne, but had spent her childhood holidays roaming the long, pristine beaches of the Surf Coast. And so, in 2015 they started to build their timber home — initially inspired by Glenn Murcutt's Marie Short farmhouse in Kempsey, NSW, and the Hill Plains Cottage by Wolveridge Architects. The house was always destined to become a labour of love, and was not as simple as they first imagined. "Both of us tend to get really carried away, and Michael always pushes the standards — it's always the full deal," Fran says.

The couple worked with Melbourne-based Nick Byrne of Byrne Architects on the home's design. "Nick is known for his striking clean lines and sculptural angles — we took his vision and gave it a rustic edge with the ironbark hardwood timber, and it went from there," Fran says. "Michael had also started to stockpile the Oregon he was pulling out of buildings in the city."

The exterior of the house takes aesthetic cues from the vernacular slab hut and sits alongside a second building, a large shed that includes the laundry and TV breakout area. The two buildings are joined by a driveway canopy and on approach, the tranquil landscape beyond is perfectly captured between the house and shed. "The idea was that you drive into the property and have a picture-frame view down the hill," Fran says.

Inside, Fran describes the home as "modern rustic" — rooms are enveloped in natural textures and tones of aged timber, contrasting with the angular sculptural concrete chimney that functions as both flue for the wood-burning heater and a room divider. "It's an art piece in itself," says Fran, who wanted to showcase the home's timber tones.

"I've never worked with so much timber before — timber that's not very consistent and has had a former life. At the moment we don't have any art on the walls because it's like the house is the art," says Fran. "We are into natural materials that move and breathe with you as the house grows old. We feel it's alive and it has quite a physical effect on you, as opposed to just a visual. Michael's priority was to build something really beautiful and visual. It has morphed into its own thing — it's not just a little shack; it's a house with its own identity."

It took two years to build the house, which included the couple choosing fittings and furnishings with the help of interior designer Lisa Buxton. "My vision for the interiors was about letting the timber be the hero, and adding some lighter colours to brighten the darker spaces," says Fran. "The view is the painting on the wall and you can sit in front of a roaring fire and look at it all day."

When the family is on the farm, they spend much of their time outdoors, heading out across the paddocks where they run a mob of Murray Grey and Angus cattle with their neighbours. "Woody is obsessed with feeding the cows. We have a mower with a trailer and he'll put his own earmuffs on," says Fran.

"There's space for him to run around and something interesting to see every time we come down. The other day a fox came down to the dam to steal the duck eggs.

"Michael is pretty much riding the lawnmower or on the tools the whole time, or will potter around and do the gardening; whereas I like to enjoy the view and read a book — which is why it suits me perfectly!"

Originally published in Country Style, February 2019.

Fran and Michael at their "modern rustic" home where timber is the hero.

The striking concrete chimney functions as a flue for the Cheminées Philippe fireplace, as well as a sculptural room divider that contrasts with the timber interior. Large windows frame the view of the paddocks and the state forest beyond. The Joe Deep sofas are from MCM House and the grey and blue cushions are from Hale Mercantile Co. The Atlas rug is from Armadillo and Co.

A trio of custom leather pendant lights from Lighting Collective sits above polished concrete benchtops in the kitchen. Leather handles from MadeMeasure, Cotto tiles from Eco Outdoor and a Falcon oven create a relaxed yet elegant look.

In the second bedroom, the lanterns are from The Society Inc; the chair is from Modern Times. **CLOCKWISE, FROM BELOW RIGHT** The main bathroom features a bath and basins from Natural Stone Bath Factory; the bench is made of recycled ironbark. The entry's storage is made of Oregon.

"WE ARE INTO NATURAL MATERIALS THAT MOVE AND BREATHE WITH YOU AS THE HOUSE GROWS OLD."

The exterior is weathering to soft grey, complemented by a vintage industrial galvanised French bath and dolly bins housing olive trees from Fossil Vintage. The outdoor setting was found on Gumtree. **FACING PAGE** An upstairs bedroom with an Armadillo and Co Ghan rug and a chair from Leonard Joel Auction House.

The grass-covered hills that have made South Gippsland, in Victoria's south east, a major dairy farming region.

Ava and Millie Mould take their pet poddy calf, Puddles, for a walk at their family's farm, Mount Koroite, near Coleraine. **FACING PAGE** The family dog, Maisy, relaxing on the verandah at the 1860s homestead.

HOME

MEGAN AND PAUL MOULD

COLERAINE VICTORIA

MOST PEOPLE WOULD find it hard to pack up a much-loved family farm, say goodbye to a familiar community and start all over again interstate. But in 2014, that's what Megan and Paul Mould did with their children, Harry, now 14, Ava, 10, and eight-year-old Millie. At the time, they were farming Hereford beef on a 5000-hectare property north-east of Tintinara in South Australia, but there were several factors at play in their decision.

"It's not something you do lightly, but we were looking for country with a higher reliability of rainfall and carrying capacity. To be able to move to a much smaller property, running the same amount of stock, is a lot easier for a family unit to run," says Megan. "We were also looking for an area where there are good education opportunities for our children, and a well-serviced centre with proximity to markets. It was really a combination of things to benefit our family."

They had already pinpointed the region around Hamilton in south-west Victoria and had been looking for a while when Megan's sister, Sally Jarvis, who lives at Balmoral, north-west of Hamilton, sent them information about a farm for sale at nearby Coleraine.

"We thought it looked like a beautiful property and home but we didn't look at it seriously," says Megan. "We had a bit of a laugh because the home looked so big and magnificent, but it was lovely and we thought, 'Wouldn't it be nice to live there?'" In the end, they decided to look at the place, and, as Megan says, "the rest is history".

Mount Koroite is 966 hectares of rich dark soil, of red gum plateau and hills running down to the creek. It's located five kilometres east of Coleraine and about 30 kilometres north-west of Hamilton. The original homestead was built in the 1860s, and then added to in grand Queen Anne style after 1911 on the winnings of the then presiding owner's horse, The Parisian, in the Melbourne Cup. Megan, 43, remembers clearly the first time she and Paul, 50, walked into the house.

"We stepped into the hallway and it was just like an envelope around us," she explains. "It's a really big home with high ceilings and big rooms, and it felt so welcoming — I was quite emotional when I was walking around it. I felt like I'd come home."

Megan had grown up on a station just outside Broken Hill, in NSW, and Paul on family pastoral properties north of Port Augusta, in South Australia. "I grew up in an old station homestead, and this home had a familiar feeling, the same smell that old country homes can have," says Megan.

Meanwhile, Paul had a similar reaction to the farming land, as Megan explains, "It had been a great spring that year and there was a lot of feed, the stock was healthy and the fences were pretty good. My husband fell in love with the farm and was getting a little excited about the possibilities there. It just ticked all the boxes."

When they finally moved in, Megan had doubts whether they'd have enough furniture to fill the big rooms. But that hasn't been a problem, thanks to handed-down family pieces and the fact she and Sally run a small business, Limewash Vintage, finding and rehoming old wares, furniture and collectables.

"I love having a revolving collection of furniture going through my house, changing it around, putting it in different rooms, and then something else will come in for a few days or weeks," says Megan.

The house was in good order and the couple felt its imperfections gave it character and warmth. However, the previous owner's departing advice was well heeded. "She told Paul he had to update the kitchen for me, and he was keen for that to happen."

Megan describes Paul as "a staunch Hereford man", who intended to carry on with the breed at Mount Koroite. But they bought a herd of Angus with the property, and then the opportunity arose to breed Angus crossed with Wagyu, which is proving successful. "When you change a farming business, you have the opportunity to do something a bit different to what you've previously done, and we are really enjoying it."

With the children now at school in Hamilton, Megan loves nothing more than getting outdoors and working with Paul. "I will often be out in the paddock, especially this time of year when it's warm and there's lots of feed, and I think how lucky we are to be living where we do," she says.

Megan adds that, while both she and her husband would have loved to still be living in that pastoral country on stations where they grew up, if they couldn't do that, then they're quite happy here where there's security and the best opportunities for their children.

"It was a hard decision to leave a family property, but this is what we chose and we're so fortunate to come to an area with great variety and fantastic welcoming people," she says. "We have been able to make friends quickly, as have our children. We love the whole lifestyle here, and the farm is a pleasure to run as well."

Originally published in Country Style, February 2018.

A photograph of one of their last Hereford bulls, by Karla Northcott, hangs above an old pigeonhole cupboard in the kitchen.

"I OFTEN THINK HOW LUCKY WE ARE TO BE LIVING WHERE WE DO."

Millie (left) and Ava, with beaglier Maisy in tow, head for the front door of the homestead.

A nook outside the mudroom. **FACING PAGE, CLOCKWISE, FROM TOP LEFT** Megan and Paul and their kids, Ava, Millie and Harry; old theatre seats sit under the Kondoolka sign, the property where Paul grew up; Ava and Millie with Puddles at the stable; ornate fretwork in one of the main rooms. The round table was given to the family by Megan's cousin.

KONDOOLKA

Tall windows with voile curtains to soften the light look out to the verandah from the bedroom. **FACING PAGE, CLOCKWISE, FROM TOP** The rear courtyard between the original 1860s wings; the main bedroom. The bedhead is from Relax and Entertain, in Warrnambool, and the bed linen from Provincial Home Living; Millie with Nibbles the lamb.

A Murray Grey heifer at the Edgar family's farm in Kudardup, WA. **FACING PAGE** Kristy and Ashley Edgar with their sons Henry and Toby.

PEOPLE

KRISTY AND ASHLEY EDGAR

CATTLE FARMERS

"WE LOVE MEETING OTHER PEOPLE THAT ALSO CARE ABOUT WHERE THEIR FOOD COMES FROM AND HOW THE ANIMALS ARE RAISED."

ASHLEY AND KRISTY EDGAR love to take their three young children down the paddock at their 24-hectare farm. Situated on Cape Leeuwin, half an hour south of Margaret River, with lush green pastures and plenty of wide open space it is an idyllic place to grow up. "It's so peaceful and the children love to help and explore," says Kristy, 36. "It makes you absolutely appreciate where we live."

With good annual rainfall and an abundance of fresh air from the Southern and Indian Oceans, the Cape region is also an ideal environment to raise their herd of sleek Black Angus cattle. Since launching Leeuwin Grass-Fed Beef seven years ago it has been "a steep learning curve" as the couple worked through the many intricacies of establishing a paddock-to-plate product.

Ashley and Kristy had set out with a vision to grass feed their cattle and rear them hormone- and antibiotic-free, using low-stress stock handling techniques. Over time their story spread and they now sell their beef throughout the South-West, with home delivery as far north as Perth.

Today the farm is a family affair with Ashley's father Ian assisting as a mentor, as well as helping with the production aspects of the business. "It is more work but it's great when customers are really excited about it," Ashley, 37, says. "I like seeing it through the whole way."

Ashley is a fifth-generation farmer who grew up on a sheep and wheat farm at Dandaragan, north-east of Perth. His parents also crayfished at Lancelin, north of Perth, and the family spent six months of the year at the coastal town, while winter months were at the farm.

Kristy, an early childhood teacher who grew up on the Central Coast of NSW, met Ashley 14 years ago while travelling overseas. After Ian and his wife Denise moved just south of Margaret River, Ashley and Kristy followed suit in 2007 and then they married two years later.

Although they now sell from the farm, as well as at Blue Ginger Fine Foods and Café in Margaret River, the Edgars initially sold their beef to a supermarket before Ashley came up with the idea to direct market it. "I was all for the idea and Ashley is pretty determined and motivated so I knew he could pull it off," recalls Kristy. "We opened the doors in December 2011."

Today, the family leases 320 hectares of land between Margaret River and Augusta to ensure year-round supply. Their cattle rotationally graze on kikuyu in the summer and rye grass and clover in the winter.

"We love meeting other people that also care about where their food comes from and how the animals are raised," explains Kristy with a smile.

Life on the farm is busy for Kristy and Ashley, along with their children Toby, six, Henry, four, and 16-month-old Livvy. Toby and Henry are always ready to help out, and will feed the cattle with Ashley or do other jobs around the farm, including collecting eggs from the family's 10 hens and helping Kristy in the vegie garden.

"We absolutely love living here — the space and being surrounded by animals," Kristy says. "Just stepping outside to let the chooks out can mentally clear your head and you start to rely on those little pockets of peace. We are lucky to raise our children here — we can leave our doors open and they are free to climb up a tree."

Ashley also enjoys a mix of ocean and farm life since he purchased a crayfish boat. "I like that each day is varied and I'm never stuck in a rut. It shows the kids that you can do anything and see something through if you work hard."

"We live in a great community," says Kristy of the region. "People really care about what they eat. We have access to amazing food here and we buy what's in season. It's what's in your garden or at the market. Everything is off the farm — it's a nice way to live."

Originally published in Country Style, February 2019.

CLOCKWISE, FROM TOP LEFT The Edgars live in a weatherboard house; the family runs about 400 head of cattle; Ashley and Toby in the paddock; Black Angus cattle.

Ashley and Toby inspecting the cattle. "It's a safe and free place for the boys to grow up," says Ashley. **FACING PAGE** A Black Angus grazing on rye grass.

"WE ARE LUCKY TO RAISE OUR CHILDREN HERE — WE CAN LEAVE OUR DOORS OPEN AND THEY ARE FREE TO CLIMB UP A TREE."

Completely off the grid, with solar panels, a back-up generator and water tanks, this Capertee, NSW, home was a dream for Danish couple, Kristine and Michael Hansen. **FACING PAGE** The iconic rocking chair by Hans J. Wegner and the wood fire from Morsø are both Danish designs. Mille the wire-haired dachshund is also a Danish expat.

HOME

KRISTINE AND MICHAEL T. HANSEN

CAPERTEE NSW

IN DENMARK, IT'S a tradition for couples to celebrate their copper wedding anniversary (12-and-a-half years, or halfway to their silver anniversary). In a quaint but symbolic ritual, friends, neighbours and family will decorate an arch around the couple's front door — but it will only go halfway.

When Michael T. Hansen, then-Danish Consul General, and his graphic-designer wife Kristine reached this important milestone they were based in Sydney — halfway around the world — so they chose a romantic weekend in NSW's Wolgan Valley instead. Little did they know, this trip would set their family's future on a totally different trajectory. "On that weekend we just fell in love with the valley and the nature," Kristine recalls. "Those valleys and rolling hills were breathtaking — Denmark is just so flat!"

In 2009, when Michael, 45, Kristine, 44, and their two sons — Oskar, 19, and Carl, 16 — moved to Sydney, they were expecting to stay three years. Nine years later, they are still here and have built their dream home on a rugged rural block at Capertee, about 45 kilometres north of Lithgow, west of the Blue Mountains.

It was after the Wolgan Valley weekend that the entire family started visiting nearby Capertee to indulge their inherent Danish desire to be outdoors. On long family walks they explored the spectacular valley, known for its dramatic escarpments, sandstone cliffs and abundant wildlife. They soon learnt of a block of land that was up for sale, but it wasn't until two years later, in 2014, that they finally managed to purchase it. "We stayed in local cabins on the weekends, getting to know the area," Kristine says of this time. "It gave us a real sense of the best position for the views and the light."

A chance meeting led the couple to architect Joe Snell, who coincidentally had studied at The Royal Danish Academy of Fine Arts in Copenhagen. "Because he's married to a Dane, we immediately connected with him," Kristine says. "We told him our dream of being totally off-grid and incorporating the craftsmanship of Australia with Danish design and simplicity, so he helped us implement that."

Situated eight kilometres from Capertee village and accessed via a winding dirt road, The Barn (which means 'the child' in Danish) is perched on a windswept hill with panoramic views of World Heritage-listed wilderness. From their deck, the family can watch kangaroos and wild goats graze among the rocky outcrops and eucalypts that punctuate the craggy landscape (until Mille, their 10-year-old wire-haired dachshund, sends them scampering as she heads off on her solitary adventures).

Just five metres wide but 35 metres long, The Barn is simplistic and sensitive to its surroundings. "It's inspired by how Danish children would make a house," Kristine says. "It's basically a box with a roof pitched at 45 degrees — that's what we have in Denmark; otherwise, the snow gets too heavy and your roof will collapse."

Double-glazed glass windows by Australian company Rylock frame the incredible views from either end of the home, while light floods the elongated interior, thanks to 19 Danish-designed Velux skylights (these skylights also help with cross-ventilation in summer). "We can lie back and watch the stars at night," Kristine says. "That's one of the reasons we love it out here — because you are closer to the sky and can see the stars. You just feel smaller, and your troubles seem smaller, too."

Inside, a highlight of the home is the custom timberwork by Capertee carpenter Lance Owens. He used local timber to craft unique rustic elements, such as the island bench, stable door and branch handles on the sliding doors. "Lance has been amazing — he also did a lot of the metalwork," says Kristine. "I would simply give him some inspiration sheets and he would go off and bring them to life."

The whole family played a part in building the house. "Carl and Michael helped Lance in his workshop, and Oskar assembled the IKEA kitchen cabinets — he's the calm and analytical one. My main job was sweeping and keeping them all fed," Kristine says. Michael's father made the bathroom sink from Danish granite, while Kristine's dad travelled to Australia to help with building. A timber meat safe from Kristine's parents' home was transformed into a cherished memory box and now hangs on the wall by the sofa.

Kristine says the family would be devastated if they ever left The Barn, which was completed in January this year. Michael is now the managing director of Nilfisk Australia, a supplier of professional cleaning equipment, so the family are free to fill the house with more memories in the years to come.

"Now that it is finished, it's really nice to be together and do the things we want, like going for long walks and just talking to each other more... We don't have a TV; at night we just listen to music. There's something different about the time up here; it really slows you down."

Originally published in Country Style, December 2018.

Carpenter Lance Owens and 16-year-old Carl made the dining table from leftover flooring. The Series 7 chairs are by Danish designer Arne Jacobsen and the Krusning light shade from IKEA. Louis Poulsen Toldbod lamps hang above the island bench.

Creating one metal runner linking the sliding doors was not without its challenges. "It took all of us standing on milk crates to get that 19-metre piece of metal into position!" says Kristine. **FACING PAGE, CLOCKWISE, FROM TOP LEFT** An old meat safe containing art, plaster casts of the boys' hands and pottery birds; sitting above the IKEA Ektorp sofa are artworks by Kristine's aunt, who was an artist at The Royal Danish Academy of Fine Arts; Michael, Oskar and Kristine; the master bedroom looks towards Turon Gates. "We often wake up with goats or kangaroos outside," says Kristine.

"WE STAYED IN LOCAL CABINS ON THE WEEKENDS. IT GAVE US A REAL SENSE OF THE BEST POSITION FOR THE VIEWS."

The bathroom sink was made by Michael's father. The unpolished brass Circa tapware was sourced from Sussex Taps, while the bench was found in a council clean-up in Sydney. **FACING PAGE** Cushions and bed linen from Denmark feature on the bed in the main bedroom. The wall-hung La Lampe Gras lamps are from Curious Grace. Above the bed is a pair of artworks from the book *Picasso's One-Liners*.

Early morning mist just lifting from the creek flat in Blue Mountain Valley on the central Queensland coast.

Three generations of the Leckey family have lived in this 1910 homestead, situated in the Acheron Valley, 125 kilometres north-east of Melbourne. **FACING PAGE** Max and Sammy on the spacious verandah, where the family often gather.

HOME

GEORGIE AND WILLIAM LECKEY

ACHERON VICTORIA

AS SOON AS you turn in at the gate to Heatherly, a picture-book rural scene begins to unfold. There's a mob of sleek black cattle lazing under majestic red gums and a long driveway gently climbing to a brimming dam. Further along the valley is a white timber homestead wrapped with deep verandahs and surrounded by a beautiful garden.

A 400-hectare family farm, Heatherly is home to Georgie and William Leckey, and their children — Eliza, 15, and Hugh, 13. It's located in one of the most scenic parts of rural Victoria, nestled among the rounded hills of the fertile Acheron Valley, 125 kilometres north-east of Melbourne. Heatherly has been in Will's family since the 1970s. "Will was interested in farming at school and he went on to do a course in agriculture," Georgie says. "He went travelling overseas in 1991 and worked in agriculture in the UK."

Although Heatherly is primarily a grazing property, the Leckeys have an interesting sideline. Close to the homestead are 12 hectares of green tea bushes, varieties of *Camellia sinensis*, that Will planted in 2001. It's a Japanese-style green tea sold under the Two Rivers label. "The majority goes straight to Japan, with other sales in Australia and worldwide through our website."

Teenager Hugh is also a keen farmer — he runs his own mob of crossbred sheep and had about 260 lambs last year. He has also started a venture breeding Wessex Saddleback pigs. "He has two sows and recently got a boar," says Georgie. Eliza, meanwhile, is away at boarding school during the term. But whenever she's at home, she spends a lot of time at pony club and competes around the district on her grey Connemara mare, Kitty.

In 2005, Georgie started a bespoke bedhead business — Heatherly Design — in the old shearing shed out the back. Originally a cottage industry that began with Georgie making upholstered bedheads for family and friends, Heatherly Design now has a Melbourne-based showroom and workshop that is staffed by specialist upholsterers, as well as a Sydney showroom.

When it comes to home decorating, Georgie's passion is for the beautifully detailed soft furnishings she discovered in the UK in the early 1990s. "I was nannying in a home that had deep buttoning, braids and gimps," she says. "There was Colefax and Fowler 'Fuchsia' chintz fabric in my bathroom and I just adored that. I hung on to those memories, so I could recreate that look."

Georgie and Will met on a plane when returning from their overseas travels. Back in Melbourne, Georgie worked for Laura Ashley, then in the decorating department at Georges on Collins Street, and at the fabric house, Wardlaw Fabrics. While at Wardlaw, she seized the opportunity to purchase the coveted 'Fuchsia' chintz from an oversupply in a client order, and stored it away for a future project.

After they married in 1998, Georgie and Will moved to the farm. "I came into the marriage, and to this house, with soft furnishings, a glory box of cushions, and a linen-covered chair," Georgie says. The original four-room homestead was built in 1910, and Will's parents added a sitting room and a lean-to style kitchen in the 1970s. A new wing, containing the bedroom Georgie and Will now occupy, a bathroom and Heatherly's design studio, was built in the early '90s.

The couple has only recently made some alterations to the layout. "I had to get a new laundry and, as we packed our tea in there, we decided to make the space a laundry/packing room. It made sense to move the kitchen to our bedroom, as there was only a wall between it and the sitting room," Georgie says.

The wall was removed and the new kitchen, completed last year, is open to the living area. The combination of painted Shaker-style cupboards, marble benchtops, a black Belling stove and a splashback of black subway tiles give the kitchen a country feel with a modern edge. "We wanted the look of an English AGA, but chose the black Belling range cooker and a black resin sink, so the kitchen doesn't look too traditional."

Engineered European oak flooring was installed in the hall and living areas, and the fireplace has a new mantel made from red gum. Industrial-style French doors now open to the verandah and the sitting room's original windows have been replaced with much larger ones to capture the view of the surrounding landscape. "The room had smaller windows, but we wanted to be able to see up to the hills," Georgie says. "This room is all about the view."

That cherished 'Fuchsia' chintz, long ago made into curtains, now hangs in Hugh's bedroom, while fabric offcuts from Georgie's workroom have been turned into cushions. In Georgie and Will's bedroom, the elegant upholstered wingback bedhead, covered in a hydrangea-patterned linen from Designers Guild, says much about what inspires her. "In decorating, so much is Scandinavian and pared back now, and that's beautiful. But I'm a fabric girl — this is what I love."

Originally published in Country Style, May 2017.

The new kitchen adjoins the living areas, and features pendant lights from Schots Home Emporium and Carrara marble benchtops from Baltic Stonemason Professionals. Hanging above the Shaker chair is a drawing by Victorian artist Darren Gilbert. The dining table is a favourite.

Digby the cat curled up on the bed in Hugh's room, where Georgie's beloved Colefax and Fowler 'Fuchsia' curtains hang. She bought the painting of an Angus bull during a trip to Vietnam. The wall colour is Khan by Porter's Paints.

CLOCKWISE, FROM TOP LEFT An armchair from Vinnies, covered in Nina Campbell 'Braulen' linen, and a landscape by Richard Claremont. The botanical still life is by Ali Wood, while the work in the gold frame is by Will's mother, Barbara; Will and Georgie with their children, Hugh and Eliza, and dogs Sammy, Heidi and Max; the main bedroom has a Heatherly Design 'Hampton' bedhead in Designers Guild 'Cassandra' linen; the craypot in the garden is used as a drinks tray.

White 'Avalanche', pink 'Poetry' and yellow 'Tweety' roses feature in a mix ready to go to market. **FACING PAGE** Paula Bandiera (left) and Bob Horan of B&B Flowers sort stems in the shed of Paula's farm in Glenorie, NSW. Dogs Beniamino and Bentley keep close by.

PEOPLE

PAULA BANDIERA AND BOB HORAN

ROSE GROWERS

ASK ANY FLORIST who sells the best roses at Sydney's frenetic, thrice-weekly flower markets — the largest in Australia — and the answer is almost certain to be B&B Flowers. Such is the exquisite beauty of the roses Paula Bandiera and Bob Horan grow on Paula's farm in Glenorie on Sydney's rural fringe.

The daughter of Italian immigrants, Paula has lived her whole life on the family's 10-hectare farm, which is today carved into several properties. At its highest point, where the 50-year-old lives with her two daughters — Ruby, 14, and Eva, 12 — there are panoramic views across the rolling floodplains of Richmond to the NSW Blue Mountains. Paula's mother, Eliza, lives next door and all three of her sisters are just down the road.

As kids, they were put to work helping their parents grow vegetables. "It was slave labour!" Paula remembers with a laugh. "Mum and Dad had no money and Dad was a workaholic, and we had to pay for it. It was every day after school, it was every weekend."

In adulthood, Paula began experimenting with flowers, growing then-popular varieties such as carnation and stock, before, in 1995, planting her first row of roses. "My first husband's father used to grow roses," she explains. "When we separated, I started growing them. At first we did the mini ones, the spray roses, and it's just evolved from there."

Today, Paula has about 40,000 bushes, with hundreds of different varieties of hybrid tea, garden and spray roses bursting into bloom from October each year. Most thrive under the shelter of wide plastic canopies, but B&B also grows field roses — mainly fragrant David Austins — out in an open patch on Paula's mother's property.

"The field roses are where Paula got her name, really," says Bob, 42, who joined the business in 2009. "They're precarious because you're subjected to all the weather, but she was bold enough to risk it."

A former florist with more than 20 years' experience, Bob grew up in the Adelaide Hills but had been working in Sydney and was looking for an escape from city life when the opportunity to work and rent a house on the farm came up.

Bob also loved Paula's idea of selling the roses in open buckets of 50 to 60 stems, as opposed to individual bunches. The larger quantities and mixed stem lengths are ideal for florists styling events or weddings, which have always been B&B's main business.

"When we first started doing it, all the other stallholders would come around laughing at us," Paula says. "They'd say, 'Is this the old stuff? Didn't you sell it on Wednesday?' It took them seven years to get it — we went in last season and every rose grower was doing open buckets. But they've still got no idea what a rose does or when it's at its best."

Today, most roses are imported and, heavily sprayed and stressed, they don't smell much like roses and often don't open. By contrast, Paula's roses uncurl with unabashed delight, the fragrant mass of petals growing larger and more spectacular with each passing day.

"She's got it in her waters," says Bob of Paula's skill at knowing what each rose needs to be at its best. "Growing them is mainly about giving them water and feed, but it's also, at 5am, deciding are you going to spray? Do you water? Do you pick that one first because it's going to rain?"

Leaving the blooms on the plant longer is also key. "Every day I'm yelling at my workers, 'Don't pick those!'" Paula says. "If you pick a rose too tight, it won't open."

During the seven-month flowering season, Paula and Bob pick seven days a week, sorting and storing the roses in the large timber and corrugated iron shed where they have three coolrooms. Bob coordinates the orders and rises before the sun each Monday, Wednesday and Friday to truck the roses to the market.

"Our best sellers are always the scented ones, like 'Evelyn', 'Fragrant Cloud', 'Winchester Cathedral' and 'Charles de Gaulle'," she says.

Paula helps at the market twice a week and employs three other staff to assist with the picking. It's hot, demanding work and leather sleeves are necessary protection against the thorns. "It's relentless, but in a funny way, it feels like there's a lot of freedom in this line of work," Bob says. "You're not stuck answering the phone all day. I have dogs and chickens, and I can wear tracksuit pants every day!"

Plus, of course, there are the roses. "I love the way they have a cycle," Paula says. "Other flowers are stunning, but you pick them and that's it. The rose keeps changing."

"It's the total romance," agrees Bob. "Most people have a good experience — they remember the roses in their grandma's garden. It's truly a beautiful flower."

Originally published in Country Style, September 2016.

CLOCKWISE, FROM TOP LEFT
Paula at her desk; the shed on the property is more than 80 years old; Bob with an armful of David Austin 'Clare' roses; six beloved dogs roam the farm, including Beniamino, Buddha, Bentley and Bumbalina.

"THE FIELD ROSES ARE WHERE PAULA GOT HER NAME... SHE WAS BOLD ENOUGH TO RISK IT."

An open field of David Austin 'Clare' roses on Paula's mum's property. **FACING PAGE** A hybrid tea rose.

Edwina Kable in the grounds of her 1880s home on Tasmania's north coast, with her children: from left, Henry, Stirling, Saffron and Hugo. **FACING PAGE** The steps from the 'hidden' front door where Edwina and her husband Mark were married is framed by red roses, a yucca and agapanthus.

HOME

EDWINA AND MARK KABLE

FORTH TASMANIA

THE STORY OF THEIR HOUSE... IS ALSO THE STORY OF THEIR RELATIONSHIP.

OLD AUSTRALIAN HOMES often have a way of showing you to the back door when you arrive. It's a trait that reveals the way people live: practical and relaxed. Edwina and Mark Kable's home, Westleigh, built in 1880 near the flats of the Forth River on Tasmania's north coast, a little west of Devonport, is such a place.

The circular driveway takes you past established garden beds and trees, eventually ending up between the barn and chook shed. The way to the back door is across giant sandstone pavers under a covered walkway. If it was raining, you could park at one end, unload your shopping and get everyone inside without getting wet. And that was exactly the intent when Edwina and Mark decided to make the back entrance — a pair of antique French doors found in Oatlands, Tasmania — the main entrance.

It's also handy for unloading four young children — Henry, 10, Stirling, nine, Hugo, six, and three-year-old Saffron. Inside, Edwina is unpacking groceries, Hugo plays on a nearby computer and Saffron is munching a carrot. Vegetables are a regular snack: Edwina and Mark are owners, with Neil Armstrong, of Harvest Moon, Tasmania's largest fresh produce company.

"We do have a front door, but it's hidden," says Edwina. From the inside, the house looks out through a doorway framed by a yucca and red roses. "We got married here, right on this doorstep," she says. The door may be obscured but the romance of their union in a garden planted by the original owners, with views of paddocks stretching to the river and the sea, is palpable.

Edwina and Mark have known each other since childhood. Mark, from the Grose Valley in the Blue Mountains, boarded at The Kings School in Sydney with Edwina's brothers. Edwina, from Burren Junction in northern NSW, boarded at Frensham School in Mittagong. They got together in their late 20s.

"Mark was in Tasmania," she says. "He had followed his father into the vegetable industry in his early 20s and bought this house on 24 hectares. I'd been working in nursing and floristry, and travelling a fair bit, but was never a career woman. I always knew I was going to be a mother. One day, Mark rang me and asked me what I was doing. I said, 'I'm lying on the beach. What are you doing? Digging potatoes?' Two weeks later I was down here for New Year. Mark put on a Nina Simone record and walked me through the house where he'd painted every room a different colour. I just went, 'Oh, I don't think I can go home... I think you've got me for good!' By the following Australia Day we were married and just over a year later we had our first son. We've been having babies ever since!"

So the story of their house — now renovated and full of light and Edwina's artworks — is also the story of their relationship: a couple raising children healthily in a small, stable community, and who spend most of their time on the property. And while it might sound like a modern-day romance, there's a lot of practical work that underpins this partnership. There are the challenges of managing a business that employs up to 400 people, farming 2000 hectares in several locations in northern Tasmania and running 100 head of cattle. All of this means that renovations have taken more than 12 years and are tackled as individual projects.

Take, for example, the massive kitchen bench that was designed by Edwina and is the heart of the house. The cabinetry is coated with paint found in old tins in the shed. The sunlit hallway (once the laundry) is warm and welcoming, and the bedrooms are kept simple.

Edwina also finds time to manage Harvest House, their farmstay in Cressy, south of Launceston, and to grow peonies that she sells to cafés and friends. This year it's her turn to run the Forth School canteen. "Mark and I donate vegetables so the kids get a vegetable and fruit platter at 10am every day. There's broccoli, celery, carrots and a couple of different pieces of fruit on plates that go to every class and they come back empty."

Hugo has grown bored on the computer. The motorbike gear comes out and Edwina heads to the barn where the family's bikes are lined up. She kick-starts Hugo's and he's off, spinning around Westleigh's circular driveway with the dogs barking in delight.

Originally published in Country Style, April 2013.

Edwina painted the Baltic pine floor of 'the gallery', which runs between the front and back of the house, in a checkerboard pattern. The antique hops fork in the corner was a gift from Mark's mother.

In Saffron's room, the elephant pillow was a gift from her grandmother. **FACING PAGE, CLOCKWISE, FROM TOP LEFT** A painting by Edwina hangs over a sideboard in the living room; blackwood and golden elm trees shade the lawn; beachcombing finds form in a changing tableau in the gallery; clerestory windows flood light into the kitchen, where the benchtop is made from Tasmanian oak and the cabinets are painted with old paint that Edwina found in the shed.

The beach at Piermont looking towards the Freycinet Peninsula on Tasmania's east coast.

Nick Haddow among his carefully chosen dairy cows on the rich, green pastures of Tasmania's Huon Valley. **FACING PAGE** A Brown Swiss calf, one of three heritage breeds on the farm.

PEOPLE

NICK HADDOW

CHEESEMAKER AND DAIRY FARMER

IT'S A BRIGHT, warm summer day as Nick Haddow, founder of Bruny Island Cheese Co, drives down onto the river flats of his new farm where the mighty Huon flows through this verdant valley in southern Tasmania. Stopping at one of the hot-wired enclosures, he ushers the way in to where his pride and joy — a small herd of dairy cows — are munching on the rich grasses, while others, lying down, languidly chew cud in the sun. You won't find the ubiquitous black and white cows at Glen Huon Farm — this herd is made up of old dairy breeds: pretty-faced Brown Swiss, Australian Dairy Shorthorn, and the panda-eyed French breed Normande.

Making cheese in the old farmhouse way that he learnt years ago in the mountains of France and Spain has been Nick's unwavering goal. Originally from South Australia, he started Bruny Island Cheese Co at Great Bay on Bruny Island in 2003, producing a range that includes the classic curd, unpasteurised Raw Milk C2. Now owning the cows that produce the milk and the pasture they graze on is a dream come true and takes him back to the source, closing the loop in the entire cheesemaking process.

Until 2014, he and his partner, Leonie Struthers, a fashion designer, lived in an old timber home next to the cheesery with their children, Tilla, 12, and Wilkie, 10. Then in 2015, the family moved up to Hobart, an hour's drive north, for the children's schooling and for Leonie to pursue her business (the LJ Struthers label), while Nick commuted to Bruny most days. In 2016, he started Bruny Island Beer Co with head brewer Evan Hunter. "The way we make beer reflects our philosophy on how we make cheese — low levels of automation, handmade, small unique batches," he says. In between all this, Nick's also made regular appearances on the SBS TV series *Gourmet Farmer* with Matthew Evans.

It was while researching his book *Milk. Made.* (published in 2016) that he started thinking about having his own dairy herd. Previously he'd sourced milk from a single herd in New Norfolk. "I visited small dairy farms in the US and Europe and realised a lot of people don't think about cheese as being a product of farming, but it is. Great cheese is made from milk that is the sum of what that cow has eaten in the past 24 hours, which makes milk — and cheese — one of the most regional products in the world. One cow, one paddock, one day is a unique combination that changes every day."

So in 2016, Nick and three business partners bought 40 hectares of Glen Huon farmland that had barely been touched for years. "We didn't have to undo anything, but on the other hand, we had to do everything." Across the river, he leased another 48 hectares from Huon Aquaculture hatchery to grow feed. "We've achieved organic certification for both properties," says Nick.

They launched a crowdfunding campaign to establish the herd. Nick found Brown Swiss at Pomborneit in western Victoria. The Australian Dairy Shorthorn were from a herd in Bendigo, Victoria. The Normande cows, a breed linked with Camembert cheese, and one bull, Nico, were from the Mount Gambier region in South Australia. On the hill above the grazing flats, a new timber-slatted dairy, built in the vernacular style of the Huon's old apple sheds, has been in operation since last September. Richard Butler, a dairy farmer who came out from Devon in the UK to become farm manager early last year, milks the 55 head twice a day — currently enough for their entire cheese production.

"We're getting 22 litres from each cow each time — you'll get 35 to 40 litres from a Holstein," Nick says. And that's the whole point — quality over quantity, he explains. The dairy is designed to be low stress for the cows, with minimal technology and automation, and a lot of manual handling. "Most dairies are built for humans, but we're not part of the real dairy industry, so we get to choose how we farm. They're not jammed in, and this operation is high labour, and for the cows there's a sense of peace and calmness."

Chickens work over the paddocks as the cows are rotated around the farm, and excess milk goes to their Berkshire and Wessex Saddleback pigs. The next stage is the building of a new cheesery on the farm. Meanwhile, a smaller cheesemaking operation will stay on Bruny, where the brewery will be expanded.

"I'd love people to swing by our cellar door, and wander through the cows to eat cheese and drink beer by the river," he says. "On the farm we'll be using indigenous moulds and yeasts as part of the maturation, and the cheese we are producing on this farm will speak so highly of location. Our number one goal is to make unpasteurised cheese, and one of the reasons we started this was to make more raw milk cheese and to have complete control over our milk. A 10-year dream has come to fruition and now we've got a 10-year project ahead of us. I want to push boundaries and I want to make cheese that represents where it's made. As a cheesemaking goal, that's kind of it for me."

Originally published in Country Style, April 2018.

The mixed herd is made up of traditional heritage milking breeds: Normande, Brown Swiss and Australian Dairy Shorthorn cows.

"GREAT CHEESE IS MADE OF MILK THAT IS THE SUM OF WHAT THAT COW HAS EATEN IN THE PAST 24 HOURS, WHICH MAKES MILK — AND CHEESE — ONE OF THE MOST REGIONAL PRODUCTS IN THE WORLD."

The centrepiece in the kitchen at Sus and Derek Bush's home, Old Bogalara, near Yass, is a table that Derek bought for $14 at a clearing sale. Pale blue Warwick fabric from Bowning Upholstery was used to cover cushions on the window seat. The colour complements the painting by Sara Cusack Cox hanging over the solid ironbark mantel. **FACING PAGE** An arrangement by Flowers From The Garden has dried out to great effect.

HOME

SUS AND DEREK BUSH

BOOKHAM NSW

A DRAMATIC ABSTRACT artwork hangs over the fireplace at Old Bogalara, the home of Sus and Derek Bush. You cannot see them, but the words of Persian poet Rumi — "I want this music and this dawn and the warmth of your cheek against mine" — are delicately inscribed into the contemporary acrylic on canvas, painted by good friend Sara Cusack Cox. The painting was a Valentine's Day gift from Sus to Derek and echoes all that they hold dear in their life at Bookham, 32 kilometres west of Yass in southern NSW.

The painting is aptly placed in the centre of the kitchen, an open and airy space under a cathedral ceiling with views to the east and west. Featuring a large window seat, butler's pantry, charming old-fashioned meat safe and long servery table, it's an inviting room that lends itself to occasions, from family dinners and quiet Sundays to bubbly parties.

While builders from Yass did most of the structural work, Derek cut and installed the second-hand herringbone floor by hand. When Sus couldn't find suitable cabinetry, she asked the manufacturers to leave part of the cupboard unlaminated so that she could add her own style and colour. The couple say it is their final addition to their unconventional home.

"I love this house, mostly because it was built on the smell of an oily rag," says 52-year-old Sus. "The kitchen is the only part we didn't scrimp on. We decided we'd have a grown-up kitchen with grown-up stuff and I chose the artwork because it's very special to have a piece of art when you are connected to the artist. Sara is forever in my kitchen."

When Sus married Derek, now 50, in 1992 and moved to 40 hectares of land at Old Bogalara, their home was a mere tin shed with a lone eucalypt keeping guard. "When Mum and Dad saw where I was going to live I think they wondered why they had spent so much time and money on my education, just for their daughter to live in a tin shack in the middle of a paddock," Sus says with a laugh. "But I believed in the family rose business and I was excited to be part of that; the house always had, and still has, a warm presence. I can't explain it but I have always loved it here."

Their primitive tin shack provided a humble starting point for the creation of a truly custom-made five-bedroom home. "The cottage just evolved over time. There wasn't a plan, really; we did what we could afford at the time," explains Sus. "We are very good recyclers. No doors match!"

The bedroom wing was added as their family grew: eldest daughter D'Arcy was born in 1994, Jock in 1996 and Max in 1998. The hallway connecting the bedrooms was used as a cricket pitch by the children and now holds photos remembering those times. "We have happy memories of dragging the children to Coonamble [in western NSW] and salvaging timber, doors and windows from a falling-down homestead owned by my parents," Sus says. "It all has beautiful connections for me."

But it's not just a family home the couple has built at Old Bogalara. When the newlyweds first moved to the property, they also took with them the flower business, Bush Roses, that Derek's mother Dee had established on the family's sheep property at nearby Bowning. They relocated the entire rose farm, including a shed, coolroom, wooden greenhouses and 5000 rose plants.

"It was a massive undertaking," recalls Sus. Growing roses is not for the faint-hearted; for nine months of the year, Sus and Derek spend seven days a week picking and packing roses in the greenhouses. They have over 20,000 hydroponically grown hybrid tea roses, all bred for cut-flower production. Valentine's Day is their busiest time. Although there's plenty of unmet demand for Australian roses, they are happy with the current production levels. "We've talked about getting bigger but I just like the idea of us working together. We're getting better at it all the time."

When Sus can manage some time away from the rose business, she loves to spend it in her own garden. Her two dogs by her side, she's constantly dreaming up new designs. "Every season and every year gives me different ideas and I love that it keeps me interested and fit," she says. The garden is rambling in parts, with vines creeping over the house, while there are also formal areas, such as the paved courtyard with a waterlily pool surrounded by manicured walls of jasmine.

A sweetener to their long working days is the surplus roses from their business, which the couple love to share with family, friends and the close-knit residents in Bookham. "The Bookham community is family," says Sus. "The people here and the land and the history are magical."

"It's nice to have a business where you can give a bit away and be a bit generous," adds Derek. Sus nods, then smiles when she says, "I'd love to know how many babies have been born because a bunch of our roses went somewhere!"

Originally published in Country Style, June 2019.

Derek and Sus in the garden with Georgie the golden retriever.

The kitchen floorboards came from an old nursing home and were painstakingly refinished and individually laid by Derek. **FACING PAGE, CLOCKWISE, FROM TOP LEFT** Derek and Sus with dachshund, Beans, their son Jock, 23, a student in Canberra, and daughter D'Arcy, 25, an artist; the meat safe in the kitchen came from Sus's parents; a cubby house built for the children years ago still stands in the garden; Georgie waits by the door.

"I LOVE THIS HOUSE, MOSTLY BECAUSE IT WAS BUILT ON THE SMELL OF AN OILY RAG."

A bedspread from Merchant Campbell in Yass. **FACING PAGE** The silverware in the bookcase has been handed down. Sus believes the fabric on the window seat is a discontinued design from Sanderson.

Bill Bryson
J.V. JONES
JAMES PATTERSON
COLIN FORBES
DIANA GABALDON
COMPLETE BOOK OF COOKERY
ILLUSTRATED GUIDE TO GARDENING
AUSTRALIAN SHOWBIZ
Beatrix Potter
COARSE FISHING
THE ENCYCLOPEDIA OF FISHING

Mount Feathertop (left) and the Bogong High Plains (right) are hidden by cloud in this view from the Great Alpine Road, near Mount Hotham in the Victorian Alps.

In Jeff O'Hare's Daylesford home, Goodman House, the main sitting room features a French stone mantel with a pair of Limoges fruit plates, green Chinese vases and bedside lamps that belonged to his mother. The painting is *Women's Journey*, from an artist in Utopia, NT. **FACING PAGE** Jeff with a former congregational organ and the painting *Night Time Industry At Altona* by Australian artist Michael Durkin.

HOME

JEFF O'HARE

DAYLESFORD VICTORIA

FATHER JEFFREY O'HARE was just a young school leaver when he took advice that stands him in good stead today. "Melbourne's Archbishop Woods said I was too young to be a priest," he says.

So, putting theology studies on the backburner and with his parents' encouragement, in 1980 he headed off for a gap year in Scotland, where he took a course in interior design at the Edinburgh College of Art. While there, he also worked with noted Edinburgh design firm Remus Interiors. When Jeff returned to Melbourne, he studied interior design at the Royal Melbourne Institute of Technology, followed by two-and-a-half years with the interiors firm Riddell Marly. Only then, in 1985, did he start his theology degree.

Entry into the Anglican Church, however, didn't end his love affair with interiors. Far from it. "I continued with several wonderful clients, and being a priest and a designer was very manageable," he says, adding that over the years he also refurbished his own homes.

It was in the mid-1990s, when he was the vicar of Romsey, that he first visited his now beautifully restored Daylesford home, Goodman House. "One of my parishioners grew up in this house and we came to visit her mother," Jeff says. "I said to her mother, 'If you ever want to sell this house, let me know.' She died in 1999 and I did the funeral, and then the family had the wake in the house."

Three months later, with the family's blessing, Jeff was the proud owner of the timber house in the spa country town 90 minutes north-west of Melbourne. The house had been built in nearby Hepburn Springs in 1890, and moved in one piece to Daylesford in 1910. It had hardly been touched since then.

"It was in need of a lot of work, but pristine in that it had the original kitchen sink and a wood stove," Jeff says. "It was the classic granny's house with gingham curtains, Wilton rose carpet and walls mostly covered in hessian and wallpaper. Out the back the stables were still in place. The garden had been planted in the 1930s and was beautiful."

According to Jeff, he collected the keys, bought a crowbar at the hardware store and immediately started demolishing clinker-brick fireplaces. He tore down wallpaper to reveal the smooth, honey-coloured Baltic pine lining boards, and pulled up kitchen lino and carpets. In a word, he stripped the house to a shell.

Jeff opened up the house with internal french doors and installed a large bay window in the dining room. At the back of the house, a timber-lined vestibule was retained, given a fresh coat of paint and fitted with a new door to the garden that had once graced a shop in London's Strand. The adjacent box room became a laundry and dogs' room for Jack Russells, Atticus and India, and the bathroom, relieved of its shag-pile carpet, was given a claw-foot bath and retiled.

It was the old Japanese maples in the back garden that inspired the addition of a magnificent new structure — a steel-framed conservatory, with a splendid finial left over from the restoration of the 1880 Royal Exhibition Building in Melbourne. Inside, it features a wall of colourful patterned Turkish tiles, and polished concrete floors strewn with antique rugs.

"The building of the conservatory was a response to the beautiful garden," Jeff says, adding that the work scheduled to take four months blew out to two years. "It has 26 opening windows... A bottomless pit of money went into this room but I'm thrilled with it — it's the gin and tonic room!" He also restored the stables as a library, design studio and guest bedroom, and built a garden shed — actually more of a romantic folly — whose domed metal roof was inspired by the French copper weathervane he found in a nearby antiques store.

It's taken more than a decade to restore Goodman House and make it a beautifully decorated and comfortable home, one that resonates with the diverse interests and personality of its owner. During this time, it remained a weekender while Jeff continued working, more recently as a chaplain at Geelong Grammar School and then as general manager and a member of the executive team at the Brotherhood of St Laurence. His book *Brotherhood: Stories of Courage and Resilience* was published by Penguin in 2009.

In 2011 he moved to Daylesford for good, commuting to Melbourne until he resigned from the Brotherhood early last year. "I love the climate and seasons here, and I'm a great lover of going to the pub on Friday nights, so I had a long-term vision that it was to be where I retired to," he says.

Retirement plans, however, are still on hold. Jeff has not only re-established his interior design practice from his studio at Goodman House, but he's also the current vicar at Daylesford's Christ Church.

"I'm doing four days in the parish — and the rest is design work that I weave in and out. And I would happily say that they're both full-time jobs!"

Originally published in Country Style, April 2015.

In the small sitting room, Jack Russell Atticus sits on a chair covered in 'Flame Stitch Tree' by Zoffany, with a Venetian chandelier and Regency fruit plates on the wall beside an abstract by Victorian painter Arch Cuthbertson.

The conservatory with its Turkish tiled walls, Regency side table and 1920s rattan chairs.

The dinnerware is 'Trapnell Sprays' from Spode and the wood stove still "cooks a good roast". **TOP LEFT** The converted stables are now a library, design studio and guest accommodation.

The dining room, lit by a generous bay window, contains a Georgian mahogany table. **BOTTOM LEFT** A pair of Italian vases from Daylesford shop Manteau Noir and a bowl of artichokes in the vestibule.

Painted in 1967, the floral still life in the hall outside the guest bedroom is by Melbourne's Florence Shirlow. **FACING PAGE, CLOCKWISE, FROM TOP LEFT** The painting above the Regency bedside table is by Bill Bevan, a protégé of Pro Hart; Jeff installed a claw-foot bath and tiled the walls himself; an unsigned painting bought at a local exhibition hangs above an 18th-century Sheridan chair; the woodshed and garden house took form after Jeff found the weathervane in a Daylesford store.

Philip starts a larger work based on a series titled Landscape Reinventions, three members of which hang on the wall beside him. **FACING PAGE** Detail from a painting in the Little World series.

PEOPLE

PHILIP WOLFHAGEN

ARTIST

"I TAKE PHOTOS OF THE LANDSCAPE — NOT ON SPECIFIC TRIPS SO MUCH, BUT RATHER COLLECTED OVER TIME."

PERHAPS IT ISN'T surprising that Philip Wolfhagen grew up to become a landscape painter. Born in 1963, he was raised on farms in Tasmania — first in the Midlands' Isis Valley and later near Longford. Rural life was always at the back of his mind, revealing itself through his paintbrush, wherever he was living.

After moving to Sydney in 1990 to study at the Sydney College of the Arts, he spent nearly six years investigating whether "there was any traction there for a country artist like me". It was here that he married Catherine, who had been a fellow arts student in Hobart (now a curator with Tasmania's Art Site Scheme). But despite making his mark in Sydney's competitive art scene, Philip missed rural living and the pair returned to Longford, 20 kilometres south of Launceston, in 1995: "I was longing for nature and wild places," he says. Soon after, their now 18-year-old daughter Hannah was born and in 2003 Theodore joined the family.

Philip has a studio in Longford and lives on an 18-hectare farm nearby with Catherine, Hannah and Theodore, Frank the cat and 18 sheep. The studio is up a rickety wooden stairway and is splendidly ramshackle, with pots of paintbrushes amid the vintage furnishings, and plaster peeling off the walls. Philip listens to music as he paints: "I started out playing Baroque vocal music but nowadays I like to play instrumental, particularly chamber, music. I use it as a way of continuity within the studio and to aid concentration. Music is kind of a silence in its own way — it can carry you along within your thoughts without interruption."

Today, Philip is one of Australia's best-known landscape painters. His works begin in memory but are ultimately imagined places, depicted with an abstraction that does not take away from their sense of presence or reality. The process begins with photography. "I take photos of the landscape — not on specific trips so much, but rather collected over time," he says. "They're just ideas and they can sit in my mind for years before I actually start working on them. And if I feel I'm lacking some other piece of the puzzle, then I go out with the camera to try and find that piece to bring back to the studio."

Returning indoors, he looks at the photographs and creates his paintings from fragments. Like the Impressionist painters of 19th-century France, Philip seeks to represent the feeling of being in a landscape rather than document what the eye actually sees; but unlike the Impressionists he doesn't paint outdoors, preferring the sanctuary of his studio.

Rather than buy ready-made wooden frames to stretch the linen for painting, Philip has turned an area of his studio over to carpentry. "I like to know the provenance of the materials I use; I've never felt comfortable buying commercial stretcher bars," he says. "I use timber that I know is grown sustainably in Tasmania, rather than harvested somewhere far away."

The predominance of greens, blues and deep, dark browns is very Tasmanian. "I think we have an interesting combination of light and weather here," he says. "We have quite English skies and yet we're at a much lower latitude than Britain. Rome and Launceston are the same latitude, 41 degrees, so the light is more reminiscent of Italian painting — and yet the weather is more reminiscent of northern Europe."

The balance of these factors underlines Philip's work in general. "When I think of the power of my work, I have to come back to music," he says. "Anyone who has studied music understands major keys and minor keys, and I see painting in that way. I strive for that in my work — attaining a balance and equilibrium."

In the end, the painting takes over, creating a life of its own in front of his eyes. "You'll hear many artists say that every painting is a world unto itself, that it has its own rules, and I think that's kind of a magical, miraculous thing. I find that it's not explainable — and it's part of the reason why painting is still meaningful. It does something that you can't do any other way."

Originally published in Country Style, March 2015.

CLOCKWISE, FROM TOP LEFT The artist with a 2014 work, *Little World No. 7*; "My studio walls are an archive of paintings retained over the years, sometimes because I love them too much or because they represent ideas that are not yet fully resolved"; updating the studio journal, a record of finished works; painting materials.

Galahs fly past Saint Carthage at Silverton, in the far west of New South Wales. The former Catholic church, which featured in the mini-series *A Town Like Alice*, has been a home to several artists in recent years.

Alice and Antony Morell's home in Victoria's Otway Ranges is set on the highest section of the property. **FACING PAGE** Reclaimed wharf timber from the Murray River is among the many recycled elements used in construction.

HOME

ALICE AND ANTONY MORELL

FORREST VICTORIA

"MY BROTHER AND I LOOKED AT EACH OTHER AND SAID, 'THIS IS THE SPOT.' "

WHEN ANTONY MORELL stumbled across an idyllic 44-hectare property near Victoria's Great Otway National Park, he found an empty shotgun cartridge and wedged it in the fork of a tree, promising himself to come back for it when the purchase papers had been signed.

"My mum's family are from Echuca and we used to go up there for holidays," Antony, a marketing strategist, explains. "We always wanted a place out of town that had a farm feel to it. I went down to the area with my brother Richard one weekend to look at a place, but we couldn't find it, so we stopped to ask for directions.

"The lady in the Forrest milk bar didn't know where it was either, but then said she happened to have three places for sale and would we like to look at them?

"The light was fading but we'd come all this way... We drove down the driveway, through the bush and there it was: the river, the five-hectare lake. It had everything my wife Alice and I wanted, and had spent years searching for: water, a flat area for horses, some bush to ride through and an area of elevated, undulating land to put a house on. My brother and I looked at each other and said, 'This is the spot.' "

Just at that moment Antony saw the cartridge. But the negotiations were protracted and by the time he returned, the sapling had begun to grow around it, leaving only a glimmer of metal.

Finding paradise for Antony, Alice and their now two-year-old daughter Raffi had taken years; buying it took 18 months, but enjoying it, says Antony, "is going to be forever".

With that in mind, the couple took their time. Rather than begin building immediately, they erected a tent with a "proper queen-size bed and frame" inside and spent a year visiting on weekends from Melbourne, getting to know the property and its surroundings.

The lovely hamlet of Forrest and the nearby national park, some two hours from Melbourne, offer a great mix of small country town and farmland stretching to thick bush, while the surf at Apollo Bay, on the Great Ocean Road, is a mere 25-minute drive away.

"We bought a heavy-duty tent with romantic illusions of me being Robert Redford in *Out Of Africa*, perched on the hill for a year," Antony recalls. "We wanted to get a sense of how the light works in summer and where the rain comes from in winter."

The plan that emerged certainly fits the landscape. As Antony proudly comments, it looks "more like a shearers' quarters than a manor house". Inside, the kitchen and living room are open plan, while a mezzanine level above contains two bedrooms and two bathrooms. The couple find the space perfect for entertaining, especially on the verandah with its view of the lake, busy with bird life.

While the shed concept was "as much for economics as it is for aesthetics" — Antony reckons the cost of the build was approximately half that of a conventional house — it's also a nod to Antony's Echuca heritage and Alice's childhood in the English countryside, filled with horses and gymkhanas. The mezzanine level sits close by the horse yard. "The horses almost feel like they're part of the family, when you wake in the middle of the night and hear them," Alice says.

The exterior is made almost entirely of recycled materials, including timber salvaged from wharves along the Murray River. "All kinds of ferries and paddleboats have probably been tethered to this wood over the years," Antony explains. The surfaces are roughly hewn and scarred, with remnant bolts trailing orange rust streaks down the wall.

"There's something magical about the way ageing corrugated iron and timber remind you of things you've seen in Australian landscapes your whole life, and that you associate with the bush in either the heat or the cold," Antony says. "At night in summer the house clicks and ticks as it cools down, and there's also the sound of the birds returning to the lake."

Alice likes her husband's passion for the space they've created: "He has put a lot of love into our homes. And, while it sounds clichéd, they do give you the love back."
Originally published in Country Style, May 2011.

The "old warhorse fridge" that Antony rescued from a family clean-out.

The combined living area and kitchen is dominated by a bison head, bought from Tarlo & Graham in Melbourne's Chapel Street. The Morells call their property Bison Lakehouse. **FACING PAGE, CLOCKWISE FROM TOP LEFT** The painting above the piano is *Hunting Dogs*, by Adam Cullen; Raffi, Antony and Alice Morell; favourite old books; the bed was made from recycled timber by a local builder.

Lal Lian in the organic garden he created near Kalangadoo in South Australia. **FACING PAGE** Red gums rise from paddocks beyond the property's orchard.

PEOPLE

LAL LIAN

ORGANIC FARMER

"IN MY OLD COUNTRY, WE NEVER HAD A DREAM — AND EVEN IF YOU HAD THEM, YOU COULDN'T GO FOR THEM."

LAL LIAN HAD never eaten beetroot before moving to Mount Gambier. Kale, spinach and parsnip were equally foreign; meals back home in Chin, a mountainous region in western Myanmar, were mainly rice and sweet corn. Now, as he harvests crops in a market garden at Kalangadoo, some 30 kilometres north of South Australia's Mount Gambier, his basket overflows with a variety of organic vegetables bound for farmers' markets, restaurants, cafés and his own family kitchen.

"Beetroot we are still not really keen to have yet, but kale we love as it's so healthy," Lal says with a smile. That luxury of choice has become one of many daily blessings for the 32-year-old since he came to Australia as a refugee in 2009. Prior to that he had spent years in New Delhi, India — having fled Myanmar at the age of 19 — where he met his wife Vika, also a refugee.

"I'll never forget my first meeting with an immigration person — I asked them to please thank the Australian Government for bringing us to a place with such freedom and opportunity," he says.

Initially settling in Adelaide, Lal was lured to Mount Gambier in 2010 by the promise of work in the horticulture industry, then received an offer beyond his wildest dreams. Kalangadoo apple growers Chris and Michelle McColl, who had previously mentored a group of Asian refugees, offered him almost a hectare of highly prized fully certified organic soil where he could produce his own crops.

"We had been cutting hay but decided that it could be put to better use; we didn't have the time to grow organic vegetables ourselves but knew the demand for them and wanted to see it happen," Chris says.

"Since I started doing this, they have very much become my backbone — how to grow, what to do," Lal says. "They have been so supportive and they are such wonderful people."

But the McColls insist it has been Lal's hard work that has led to his success. "We provide the water and the land, the mentoring and guidance in return for the weekly rent of one box of vegetables," Chris says. "We're letting him use the land, but he's doing all of the work, with hand tools only, and it has been a really rewarding experience and a privilege to get to know his family."

Lal and Vika, and their children — Miriam, four, Sarah, one, and newborn Joseph — regularly share meals with the McColls. "Michelle once made roasted beetroot, parsnip and carrots, and I asked my wife to do the same one night. She tried to do it the way they did it... never again!" Lal says with a smile.

Becoming founding members of the Mount Gambier Farmers' Market has been another way for Lal and Vika to mix with the community. "Farmers' markets are such a beautiful concept; after growing vegetables myself, seeing them start off as a tiny seed and how healthy they look — people would be so excited to see this and I really hope that they can support these markets so that growers like me can keep going."

Despite the widespread publicity about the benefits of buying organic, Lal admits that he has sometimes had difficulties trying to convince his local customers about the value. "Country people don't seem to be excited by organic vegetables, but people go crazy for them in the city — if only the cost of getting the produce to Adelaide or Melbourne didn't make it so difficult," he says.

In a bid to diversify and improve his income, Lal is now planning to study social work. It's a career he began as a volunteer among the Chin community in India, where he "waited and waited" for resettlement after escaping the political uncertainty of Myanmar. It's also a way to pay forward some of the kindness he has received in his new home.

"In my old country, we never had a dream — and even if you had them, you couldn't go for them," he says. "Here, we can have a dream for our future and while it may take us longer than others, we are willing to try. It's up to us — that's what I feel."

Originally published in Country Style, November 2013.

CLOCKWISE, FROM TOP LEFT Lal with Chris and Michelle McColl; Roma tomatoes on the vine; the farming is all done by hand; a shady spot for the harvested produce.

overs
&
akers
THE POWER OF imagination MAKES US infinite
-John Muir
COLLECTIVE
"You're not your career. You're a scientist doing experiments in the world. And the world's your lab and you should just try an experiment."
FÊTE/LIFE

The 1880s cottage on the adjoining property is home to Kirstie's parents, Cathy and Geoff, and was originally featured in *Country Style*, March 2009. **FACING PAGE** An old door that once belonged to Kirstie Penton's great-grandmother was turned into a desktop when her family got together to renovate an old courthouse for her. Clippings are a source of inspiration for Kirstie.

HOME

THE PENTON FAMILY

MERINGANDAN QUEENSLAND

THERE'S ALWAYS A moment during a renovation when you wonder if the hard work will ever pay off. For Kirstie Penton, that moment came while she was high on a scaffold with her younger brother, Andrew, and father, Geoff, ripping down pieces of the old ceiling from the Meringandan Courthouse, dust falling down on them.

"I had goggles on but my face was black," Kirstie says with a laugh. "You don't really know what you're going to find, but it was even better than we imagined."

Eighteen months on, when Kirstie enters that room of the former courthouse about 20 kilometres north-west of Toowoomba, it's the exposed beams and high-pitched ceiling — previously hidden — that capture her attention. "Every time I walk in, I take a deep breath and have an 'a-ha' moment," the 24-year-old says. "It was definitely a family effort and we've really worked hard for what it looks like now."

Kirstie had originally wanted to paint the beams white but was outvoted. "I'm grateful now that we kept them," she says. "The majority rules in this family!"

Her parents, Cathy and Geoff, purchased the courthouse, which neighbours their 1880s railway cottage in the small country town, 11 years ago. "We were worried someone would buy it and knock it down as it was in really bad disrepair," says Cathy. "We didn't really have the money at the time but we thought, why not? We knew it could be beautiful again."

Once part of Gowrie Station, the Meringandan area was resumed and opened for selection in 1872. Meringandan was the first station on the railway line from Toowoomba to Cabarlah, and the Cabarlah Courthouse was shifted to Meringandan early last century as the farming area grew.

The Pentons put tenants into the adjoining living area of the courthouse — once the police officers' quarters — and initially used the large open courtroom for storage. When Kirstie, who works in Toowoomba as a senior academic program support officer at the University of Southern Queensland, decided to move back home, it was the perfect opportunity to focus on the room, which measures eight by four-and-a-half metres.

"We knew it was going to be Kirstie's apartment so we wanted to restore it to its former glory," says Cathy, who makes charms and embroidered cushions from her studio in the railway cottage under the label Cathy Penton Atelier.

After re-roofing and re-stumping the building and removing the low ceiling, Cathy, Geoff, Andrew and Kirstie painted the walls in Dulux's Antique White USA and sanded the painted hoop pine floor, before sealing it with Woca oil.

"I remember sitting on the floor with a chisel trying to get the red shiny stain out of the grooves," Kirstie says. "It did not want to budge and there were some days you wished you could blink your eyes and it would be done. My love is the painting, not so much the prep work!"

Kirstie and Geoff found a thick timber board at a salvage yard in Toowoomba, which they had planed in half and sanded then installed as shelving in the kitchen. Geoff, who is the chief executive officer for the Queensland Murray-Darling Committee, enjoys woodwork in his spare time and also built the vanity in the bathroom, which is tucked behind the low wall of the kitchen.

Cathy and Kirstie selected handless cabinetry, stone benchtops and a butler's sink from IKEA to create a sleek look for the kitchen, where Kirstie displays her collected ceramic ware. With a shared love of decorating, the mother and daughter duo enjoy shifting things around and bouncing ideas off each other. "It's minimal but with warmth," says Cathy. "Kirstie likes to put a bit more new in while I tend to use what I have and build on that... she has a great eye."

Kirstie has used pallets as a base for her bed, which makes good use of the space and allows a view over the open living area. "It looks cool and doesn't cost anything," she says.

With the interior complete, Cathy chose Dulux matte black for the exterior and planted a rosemary hedge around its perimeter. Kirstie moved into the courthouse a year ago and regularly strolls up the hill, past their pet sheep and the rolling farmland, to her parents' house for dinner. Andrew, who is studying physics two hours away in Brisbane, gets home as much as possible. "Because Geoff travels so much, Kirstie and I often watch a show together or have dinner. My daughter is one of my closest friends in the world," says Cathy.

Kirstie now has the renovators' bug and is already thinking of her next project.

"I think this is amazing and I'm saving up to find another old place that needs some love in the future to keep it going. How incredible that my parents were able to do this for me; it's very special."

Originally published in Country Style, November 2017.

Kirstie's sleigh bed at her parents' home was crafted by her dad Geoff, who also made the shutters from a chance find of old corrugated iron.

A view of the side door of the courtroom from the former police officers' residence. **FACING PAGE, CLOCKWISE, FROM TOP** The exposed beams are the feature inside the courtroom; Kirstie with her mum Cathy on the front steps of the old courtroom, which Kirstie now calls home; one of the Pentons' pet sheep.

The brumbies of Coffin Bay in South Australia are a direct link to the Eyre Peninsula's colonial past.

The original fireplace in Emma and Angus Graham's 1820s homestead has been restored with a European oak mantel, while the couches are from Coco Republic. **FACING PAGE** Emma, with Graphite, one of the family's horses.

HOME

EMMA AND ANGUS GRAHAM

BINALONG NSW

A RICH VEIN of Australian folklore runs through southern NSW's Binalong district and Mylora, an historic homestead in the area, features in many tales regaled by locals. It is immortalised in one of Banjo Paterson's first published poems *The Mylora Elopement*, based on his memories growing up on the neighbouring property, Illalong. However, the property also has links to less reputable characters, and it's these stories that often attract the most intrigue.

Mylora's previous owners were the Garry family, whose ancestors were early pioneers of the area. During the 1850s gold rush, hold-ups were common on the Cobb & Co route flanking the outer reaches of the property, as bushrangers sought their fortune with pistols rather than pickaxes. Local legend has it that after robbing a mail coach, notorious outlaws Johnny Gilbert and John Dunn stole two valuable racehorses from Mylora. But Mrs Garry's jewels remained untouched, cleverly concealed under a brooding hen.

For Mylora's current owners, Angus and Emma Graham, these stories add another layer of history to their already charming home, located about 34 kilometres north-west of Yass. Built in the 1820s, the stately stone house with formal dining room, sitting room and five bedrooms sits amongst the well-established leafy garden with a tennis court, pool and manicured lawns. Emma says local tales added to the allure when she first came to Mylora. "It's made me fall in love with it even more," the 36-year-old explains.

Compared to the Garry family, Angus and Emma have only lived at Mylora together for a relatively short time. Shortly after their first child Hunter was born in 2016, Emma, a former marketing manager, moved to Mylora full-time. About a year later, Angus and Emma were married in the homestead's impressive garden.

"We had six inches of rain but it was the most spectacular day," says Emma. "It stopped after the ceremony and we were able to have drinks and canapés in the beautiful surrounds before the downpour started again!"

Angus, 48, has a longer history with the district, having grown up nearby at his parents' Galong farm, Argyle. In 1999, he moved to Mylora when his family purchased the 3200-hectare property in partnership with an investor. "I've lived at Mylora for over 20 years and it's the place I feel most at peace. I get a strong sense of calm here," says Angus (or 'Gus' for short). "In times of stress I'll ride to the top of the hills and take it all in."

In between the demands of the farm and his family, which includes Hunter, two-and-a-half, and Sinclair, three months, as well as two children from his previous marriage, Sophie, 16, and Oliver, 15, Angus manages to find time for the ongoing restoration of the homestead.

"Gus is hands-on and hard yakka but there's a bit of a romantic side to him in terms of idealism," says Emma. Testament to this passion, Angus was searching for the perfect floorboards for the new open-plan living area a few years ago when he discovered a Sydney business importing reclaimed European oak. He was so taken with the floorboards, and the story behind them, that he ended up buying the business. Today, Woodstock Resources sells reclaimed timber and other items salvaged from old buildings, barns and railways from France, Belgium, Serbia, the Netherlands and Turkey.

As the business started to grow, Angus began storing oak beams, gates and chandeliers in the sheds at Mylora. "One day he said, 'We can't sell a secret,' and it made complete sense to start thinking about a new retail space closer to home," says Emma.

In 2017, Woodstock Resources opened a concept store at Jugiong, about 30 minutes' drive south-west of Mylora. "We created a retail shop using natural materials — leather, wool, linen, oak, stone, antler and glass. People always comment about how great the smell is and how calming the space feels."

Occasionally Mylora serves as a showroom, too. "The living room has been completely opened up and the ceiling lifted, and now it's this beautiful space," Emma explains. "Our reclaimed European oak herringbone floor from a barn in Romania runs the entirety of the room and elevates the feeling of expanse."

The family spend most of their time in this open-plan space and have installed mechanical fly-screen blinds to enclose the nearby verandah. "It's the most perfect spot for a casual summer drink. You can see the creek and hear the sounds of the birds and still get an idea of what's happening outside," Emma says.

For the children, the property is a natural playground where they can explore with their horses and play on the old river-gum slab table, which also plays a part in the folklore of Mylora. "The Garry family would always invite lots of the community there for a picnic at Easter, and so every June long weekend we have a super-casual bonfire barbecue down there, where anyone who's around comes along with their kids," says Emma.

Originally published in Country Style, May 2019.

For their kitchen, Emma and Angus sourced a marble benchtop for the island from Carrara Marble and Granite in Sydney and Tonalite subway tiles for the splashback from Tiles by Kate. The recycled European oak floorboards are from the couple's business Woodstock Resources.

The bedroom's reclaimed Woodstock Resources floorboards came from a railway station in Paris. The bedlinen is from Sheridan and the striped cushions are Libeco. The old wicker chair was picked up at auction. **FACING PAGE, CLOCKWISE, FROM TOP LEFT** Angus says the property's stunning gardens "seem to manage themselves"; Angus with Hunter on one of his horses; the expansive gardens include a pond; the ram's head art piece called 'Stanley' is by Sarah Bishop.

The Gothic Revival stables at Shene Estate in Tasmania's Southern Midlands, built in 1851. **FACING PAGE** Myfanwy with her parents, Anne and David, plus terrier Rupert Archibald

PEOPLE

MYFANWY KERNKE

GIN MAKER

IT WOULD BE hard to imagine a more fairytale setting for a wedding than the magnificent stone farm buildings at Shene in Tasmania's Southern Midlands. And such was the case for Myfanwy Kernke when she married theatre director Ben Schostakowski at Shene in December 2014. After friends and family had gathered for the reception in the former barn, they formed an archway beneath the imposing stable edifice for the couple's departure. The event also marked new life and purpose for the historic buildings, to the joy of Myfanwy's parents, Anne and David Kernke. The couple bought the crumbling estate, one of Tasmania's earliest and most important heritage-listed pastoral properties, in 2007 and since then have worked hard to restore the buildings.

"It was a very special and emotional day," says Myfanwy, the 27-year-old events manager at Shene. "I know so much about the buildings and to see everyone come into the barn to celebrate such a milestone in our lives, and to have such joy in the buildings after they had been in such a terrible state — I still think about it every day!"

The Shene stables make an impact even from afar. Travellers passing Pontville, about 30 minutes' drive north of Hobart, have long been struck by the imposing Gothic Revival-style building. It certainly caught the attention of Anne and David, inveterate renovators of classic tin and timber houses in their hometown of Ipswich, Queensland, who were looking for a change and a challenge.

"In my childhood I was dragged through every heritage property in Queensland," Myfanwy recalls. "Mum and Dad are restoration addicts who left their mark on the streetscapes where we lived."

Anne and David fell in love with Tasmania and its heritage buildings on a holiday in the late 1990s. "We saw that Tasmania had the finest colonial buildings in Australia," Anne says. "We went back to Queensland while the kids were still at school and then we started looking, mainly on the internet. We saw this and it was a one-off, a mystery place. We could have had a house on the waterfront, but this property was under threat of subdivision at the time, and that would have been awful."

The vast stables were built in 1851 by successful lawyer and businessman, Gamaliel Butler. They encompass horse stalls, a coach house, a harness and tack room, grooms' quarters, a granary and a small upstairs chapel for the convict workers. A tower was never finished and still awaits a roof. Alongside is a barn that in latter years was used as a shearing shed, and nearby is the original Georgian sandstone homestead that was built in several stages from the 1820s to the 1850s.

The Kernkes embarked on the massive restoration, employing teams of artisans including stonemasons. They corrected drainage problems, rewired, and replaced floors, windows and doors with accurate replicas of what would have been there originally. In 2013, Myfanwy, who worked at Brisbane's La Boite Theatre Company, joined her parents at Shene. Her younger sister, Ceridwen, still lives in Brisbane.

For the family, Shene has become a consuming passion. "You don't clock off, " Myfanwy says. "And when we come in at night and watch the BBC's *Country House Rescue* on the ABC, we scream at the screen, 'The drainage, the drainage!' "

Shene slowly revealed some of its secrets. After discovering the remnants of lead in the tower window frames they reinstated leadlight windows. "All the houses had leadlight windows," Myfanwy says. "And we know that John Glover, the famous early colonial artist, painted *The Bath of Diana* and *Aborigines Dancing at Brighton* in one of the paddocks."

Today the family, who also run a few cattle and crossbred sheep on their 12 hectares, open Shene for small group tours. There's an artist residency program and concerts, weddings and musical performances held in the barn. "It's so lovely to see people pouring in to hear 18th-century chamber music in the barn, in a place where they once had horses," Myfanwy says.

Later this year they'll open a gin and whiskey distillery behind the stables, and Myfanwy says there's evidence that gin was Mr Butler's preferred beverage. "We unearthed glistening shards of old Dutch Case gin bottles and beautiful old torpedo tonic water bottles just off the homestead verandah," she says. "So we're dedicating the gin distillery to him."

And early this year the sound of hooves on flagstones returned to Shene when it became the headquarters for Hobart Polo Club, with a playing field laid out before the stables. "We now have a functioning tack room and it's lovely to see horses back on the site," Myfanwy says.

Shene's fabric may be secure, but the Kernkes still have more plans for the future. "I don't think we'll ever finish," says Myfanwy. "It's such an important site and it's equally important to tell its story. Shene has so many more tales to tell — if only the walls could talk!"

Originally published in Country Style, October 2015.

"Mr Hoover, Poppy Rose and Wellington are our pet lambs — and escape artists!" says Myfanwy. "The pail of treats is to lure them back to their paddock."

CLOCKWISE, FROM TOP LEFT The chapel for convicts on the second floor; the 1820s convict quarters have been refurbished for the artist residency program; axes in the former meat hanging room; the view south towards Mount Wellington. **FACING PAGE** Shene's events manager and gin maker, Myfanwy Kernke, in the estate's old dairy.

The newly renovated kitchen at Gerard Cook and Rachel Luchetti's barn-style family retreat in the Noosa hinterland has loads of warmth and character, thanks to timber details, as well as the Havsen farm sink and Glittran kitchen mixer, both from IKEA. **FACING PAGE** The couple relaxing on the deck.

HOME

RACHEL LUCHETTI AND GERARD COOK

DOONAN QUEENSLAND

DRIVING THROUGH THE undulating hinterland of Queensland's Sunshine Coast, a glimpse of red peeks cheerfully through a clearing in the native bushland. At the side of the road, an eye-catching letterbox provides a touch of whimsy and a tantalising hint of what's to come. Then, as your wheels crunch through the oval-shaped poinciana seeds that line the driveway, you are rewarded with the cheery sight of Little Red Barn — the much-loved abode of Sydney-based interior designer Rachel Luchetti and her builder husband Gerard Cook, who transformed a kit-home barn into a family retreat.

"Arriving at the barn is always such a wonderful feeling," says Rachel, who takes their two sons, Leonard, aged four, and two-year-old Walter, to visit at every opportunity. "As we live in an inner-city apartment, we crave the open space that it affords us."

The couple bought the picturesque property at Doonan, 19 kilometres south of Noosa, in early 2016, choosing to source as many of the materials and furnishings as they could locally. "As this is a holiday home, we couldn't justify spending much on it and had to remain quite thrifty," says Rachel, who looked to the surrounding towns of Yandina, Pomona and Cooroy for suitable second-hand pieces.

"Gumtree has been great, not only for the barn but also because you get to meet people around the area," she says. "When I've gone to pick something up, I've been able to see houses that you wouldn't normally see because they're hidden away from the main road."

Buying in this area had been a dream for a while: "We've been coming up to Noosa for a long time," says 38-year-old Rachel. "The first holiday Ged and I took together was to Noosa, so it's a special place for us. We were looking at the real estate windows and noticed there was really good value a little further from the coast. We thought we'd come up and do a recce, have a drive around, when we came across this place."

At just under one hectare, the property is perfect for this busy couple, who were looking for something semi-rural but didn't want the responsibility and upkeep of a farm. "It's not a lot of maintenance but it also doesn't feel like we have neighbours," says Rachel.

The pair wasted no time in renovating, moving up while Rachel was on maternity leave and Leonard was just two years old. "When we first bought the place, it was a kit-home barn with one bedroom and a ladder loft," she says. "It had character and wasn't overdone, but it definitely needed some updates." As a builder, 42-year-old Gerard did almost all the work himself, from concreting and laying the tiles to re-lining and insulating the internal walls. "The only tradies we had in were an electrician and a plumber," says Rachel.

The loft was extended to include a landing area, and an extra bedroom and bathroom were added downstairs. "There were a couple of weeks when it was unlivable," says Rachel. "There were gaping holes and it was really dusty." Today, all signs of dirt and disruption are gone. Rachel says the resulting double-height living space, complete with a wood-burning fireplace and country-style kitchen, were worth any temporary inconvenience.

The space now feels luxurious, with fresh white walls and touches of timber to add warmth and character. Rachel's favourite spot is the outdoor bath, accessible via the ensuite that opens onto the verandah through bi-fold doors. "To have a glass of wine in the bath and read a book — that's my dream!" she says.

A steep block meant there was also work to be done outside. "The property is at a 25-degree gradient," says Rachel. "It had no connection to the garden and was too sloped for the kids to play." Unperturbed, Gerard brought his bobcat and excavator up from Sydney and got to work building retaining walls and backfilling to create a level grassy area. He also created a circular driveway out front, lining it with the long, oval-shaped seeds of poinciana trees he collected locally.

As a holiday home, a swimming pool was high on the wish list but the limitations of the slope meant the couple had to get creative. "We were both worried about the cost of building an in-ground pool on a site like this," says Rachel, who found their concrete plunge pool at Allcast Precast in nearby Woombye. "We also wanted to get that bridge effect leading from the barn out to the pool — it was definitely a bit of work getting that right."

The pool is now the ideal place to gaze across the hinterland hills, while a nearby pandanus recreates the look of the Sunshine Coast's beaches. But though the sandy shores of Noosa are mere minutes away, Rachel says the barn has everything they need for a relaxing holiday at home.

"The boys burst through the doors to rediscover cherished toys and get busy with what they describe as 'builders' work' and repairs around the property with their miniature tools," she says. "We go to the beach early in the morning when it's not too busy or hot, then come back here and hang out all day. It's our little oasis."

Originally published in Country Style, May 2019.

Four-year-old Leonard and two-year-old Walter enjoy roaming in and around the family's holiday home.

"WE GO TO THE BEACH EARLY IN THE MORNING WHEN IT'S NOT TOO BUSY OR HOT, THEN COME BACK HERE AND HANG OUT ALL DAY. IT'S OUR LITTLE OASIS."

CLOCKWISE, FROM BELOW LEFT The pool from Allcast Precast is the perfect spot to take in views of the hinterland; freshly painted white walls and window frames, and antique bedroom furniture, sourced by Rachel on Gumtree, add to the cosy country feel. The Winchester Spindle bed is from Pod Furniture in the UK; the open-plan kitchen, dining and living area features lofty ceilings — much of the furniture was found on Gumtree, while the Jasper sofa is from King Living; the tapware in the bathroom is from Astra Walker. **FACING PAGE** The outdoor claw-foot bath was a Gumtree find; the floor-mounted tap with hand shower is from Astra Walker.

The Wooroolin Wetland, about 16 kilometres north of Kingaroy on the Bunya Highway, is popular with birdwatchers.

On a remote property 270 kilometres north of Broken Hill, NSW, Zanna and Matt Gale's home is filled with creative character, such as the windmill head art hung on the wall. **FACING PAGE** The couple stand on a sandhill on their 65,000-hectare sheep and cattle station.

HOME

ZANNA AND MATT GALE

BROKEN HILL NSW

LIVING ON A remote sheep and cattle station that's 270 kilometres north of Broken Hill can be a challenge at the best of times, but add a drought and it becomes a test of endurance. Luckily, Zanna and Matt Gale of Pincally Station are more than a match for their beloved and rugged 65,000-hectare station that the pair has called home for more than 20 years.

The couple married in 1996 after meeting in Broken Hill at the St Patrick's race day. Zanna, originally from Menindee in NSW's far west, was working as a governess on a station south of Broken Hill.

The original section of the house is almost a century old and a large living room connects to an extension built 50 years ago, with a central breezeway and rooms on either side, encased by a wide, screened verandah.

"When I first came here, it needed a good clean-up," Zanna recalls. "You couldn't even see through the windows, and dust came in everywhere. We gradually replaced the louvres with glass panes, applied plasterboard and painted the walls in off-white shades. As time went on I could see so much potential; we pulled up old lino that was glued to jarrah floorboards, and sanded and polished them."

As a result of the last 18 months of prolonged dry, Matt and Zanna have destocked to less than half of their herd, selling off lambs, wethers and cattle. They spent their days feeding the remaining livestock — the couple hope to hold onto their core breeders and have sent cattle on agistment to South Australia. "It doesn't have to rain here, as long as it rains somewhere," says Matt.

After that, the 45-year-old plans to work on fencing and water infrastructure. "I haven't had time to do that for the last eight months as all we've been doing is feeding. To come from outside into our garden and house is a comfort — you can almost shut off."

Surrounded by an olive grove, a large vegetable garden, lawns and hedges, the sprawling homestead is a leafy refuge (thanks to a desalination unit on a bore). It's home to the couple and their daughters Bella, 16, Lucy, 14, and 12-year-old Millie, who is in her final year of primary distance education, while her elder sisters are at boarding school. "It's a great space to escape from the drought," says Zanna, 43, of the renovation that was completed two years ago. "I'm lucky to have this to come home to and switch off from what's happening outside for a little while."

Over the last two decades, Matt and Zanna have gradually renovated the house, but held off overhauling the kitchen until they were sure of a way forward. "Our old kitchen was dilapidated; it was cold, dark and falling apart," Zanna explains. "The walls had been eaten out by white ants and, on one occasion, someone actually fell through the old floorboards! I wanted to give it a new lease of life without losing the original features that I love."

In the meantime, Zanna collated ideas for the kitchen design and pursued her love of interiors by studying with the International School of Colour and Design.

"My vision was to create a large, open functional space with lots of natural light," she says. "Cooking for family and station hands is a major part of life here, and I needed bench space with storage; large, open shelving; and a coolroom in the butler's pantry to keep our stores, as sometimes it's a month between trips to town."

The renovation was carried out over four months and involved demolishing a quarter of the house, with Zanna and Matt helping in between running the station. Insulation was a major consideration, as the homestead was prone to extreme weather. An open-plan kitchen and living area was created with double-glazed sliding doors, which open onto the pergola that Matt made. This links to the entertainment area, pool and courtyard.

Zanna chose simple, clean lines for the kitchen design. She added character with old timber shelves found in the shed and used a barn door to connect the area to the rest of the house. A large draftsman's table bought at an auction has become the dining table, after a stint as a workbench in the shed.

"It's old and worn and completely imperfect: just how I like it!" Zanna says. "The kitchen was actually planned around that 3.6-metre-long table."

In the other rooms are pieces Zanna has collected that reflect the character of the house and landscape, such as a heavy timber lamp base made from a piece of red gum she found in the workshop. "I've inherited my style and way of pulling things together from my mum and my grandmother. I like raw materials — and rustic, early Australian pieces really suit this house. I keep moving things around until they look right."

Despite the challenges of drought, each day brings the thrill of returning to the house after a long, dusty day in the paddock. "Now it's a place where we spend our time discussing our daily events, eating, cooking and relaxing," says Zanna. "We love sitting on the deck and getting away from it all."

Originally published in Country Style, November 2018.

The walls of the hallway are painted in Wattyl Freesia, while the floor is in Porter's Paints Perfect Floor Paint in K2.

“DESPITE THE DROUGHT, EACH DAY BRINGS THE THRILL OF RETURNING TO THE HOUSE AFTER A LONG, DUSTY DAY IN THE PADDOCK.”

Horses are an important part of life at Pincally Station. **FACING PAGE** The beautiful isolation of the outback landscape on the station.

Foliage from olive trees in the garden decorates the main bedroom, which features Mud Australia lamps. **FACING PAGE, CLOCKWISE, FROM TOP LEFT** The former draftsman's table was rescued from the workshed; the floor is a cool place for the cavalier King Charles spaniels Lolly and Eddie; the studio is a treasure trove of collected wares and art; Zanna has incorporated earthy materials and textures in the bathroom.

As oyster farmers, Dom and Pip Boyton, pictured here with their son Solomon, spend a lot of their time on the water tending to oysters and enjoying the natural beauty of Merimbula Lake. **FACING PAGE** An Australian native flat oyster called *Ostrea angasi*.

PEOPLE

PIP AND DOM BOYTON

OYSTER FARMERS

"WE'RE IN A GORGEOUS POCKET OF WILDERNESS RIGHT ON THE LAKEFRONT."

AS A TEENAGER in Year 11, Dom Boyton travelled from Merimbula on the far south coast of NSW to the Sydney Opera House for work experience in the restaurant kitchen. It was the perfect place to learn what it would take to be a chef. The only trouble was that instead of concentrating on the tasks he'd been given, he found himself looking out of the window at Sydney Harbour and dreaming of home.

"I wanted to be out there on the water," recalls Dom. "I realised I didn't want to be inside. It was a good experience though; I found out what I didn't want to do."

Dom, 41, had been mucking about on the water ever since his parents, Chris, an accountant, and Shelley, a librarian, moved their family — Dom and his older sister Samantha — from Canberra to Merimbula when they bought a 40-hectare oyster lease on the lake in the early 1980s.

Today, it's Dom and wife Pip's kids, Solomon, 12, and Eddison, 10, who muck about on the water.

"We're in a gorgeous pocket of wilderness right on the lakefront," says Pip, 35, a former chef and now a driving force alongside Dom in their oyster farming business, Merimbula Gourmet Oysters. "It's still my favourite thing to be out on the water," says Dom. "At sunrise, the birds are waking and the light is amazing."

Both Dom and Pip, who grew up in nearby Pambula just 10 kilometres south of Merimbula, left town to further their careers once they finished school. Dom studied aquaculture in Tasmania and Pip trained as a chef, but they returned a few years later. Dom worked alongside his parents on the oyster lease from 2000, and Pip joined them in 2004.

"The biggest thing I learnt when I was away was that the oyster lease could be more than a hobby; it could be a business," says Dom. While many oyster growers are content to earn an income, Dom could see potential and introduced new efficiencies, such as mechanical grading, and changed the way the oysters are grown from tarred stick and trays to floating bags and single-seed cultivation. One of this system's attributes is that it reduces the impact on the lake floor ecosystem as there are fewer posts.

Instead of receiving a box of oysters in a restaurant kitchen and having little idea how they're grown or where they're from, Pip now revels in seeing food grow from start to finish. "It was an eye-opener," she says. "I never thought I'd come home; I was going to be a chef and travel all over the world. But it was very easy to find a role here, and Chris and Shelley were very open to having me at the farm. It was hard work early on, but fun."

Even though the Boytons grade mechanically, they still go through every bucket by hand to check that only premium oysters are being sent out. "We're part of the South Coast farmer-owned company, Australia's Oyster Coast," says Pip. "That's another level of quality as those oysters go into the best restaurants and are exported. Tasting notes go into every box, and it's wonderful to make consumers aware that every oyster is different. Our notes will say where on the farm the oyster was grown — in the estuary, for example, which is sandy, or the weedy substrate — and talk about the different high notes."

"Broadly speaking, South Coast winter oysters are sweet and summer oysters, when they're getting into breeding condition, are creamier," explains Dom.

The Boytons grow Sydney rock oysters (some, known as 'plates', are grown to 70 grams — very large for an oyster) and they're one of only a few South Coast growers who produce the flat, native oyster *Ostrea angasi*. "Those are trickier," says Dom. "They don't like fresh water or hot weather, but they're becoming more and more popular." In response to erratic seasonal patterns, and in a bid to stay viable into the future, the Boytons have been looking at growing other shellfish native to the area. "We're looking at clams," says Pip. "Being native, they can cope with high seawater temperatures."

While running the farm is a daily commitment, Dom and Pip are also committed to building up the industry and are involved in a number of governmental and tourism committees and boards.

"It's important," says Pip. "Our life is oysters — the business is like our third child."

Originally published in Country Style, February 2018.

Since taking sole charge of the oyster lease, Dom has instigated changes to the operations, replacing tarred stick and trays with a floating bag system that uses fewer structural posts, reducing the impact on the floor of the lake.

A passing seagull takes a moment's rest. **FACING PAGE, CLOCKWISE, FROM TOP LEFT** Dom and Pip work closely together; oyster harvest; Dom working the lease; the Lake's seagrass provides a habitat for all sorts of sea life.

"IT'S STILL MY FAVOURITE THING TO BE OUT ON THE WATER. AT SUNRISE, THE BIRDS ARE WAKING AND THE LIGHT IS AMAZING."

The bluestone homestead. **FACING PAGE** Lucy, Annabelle, Damian and Sophie with Scout the Jack Russell on the eastern verandah.

HOME

DAMIAN CANNY

HESSE VICTORIA

DAMIAN CANNY'S LONG-TIME love of the wide open spaces and big skies of Victoria's Western District harks back to his youth. It was his early connection with the area's fertile volcanic soils, along with his appreciation for time-worn bluestone homesteads steeped in history, that drew him back to Barunah Plains at Hesse, 126 kilometres south-west of Melbourne.

Damian had known of Barunah Plains since he was a teenager, when he worked nearby as a jackaroo on the historic Mount Hesse sheep station, one of the largest merino wool producers in Australia.

"I grew up in Melbourne, but as a young boy I had visited Mount Hesse and really liked the lifestyle, the merino sheep and their wool," he says. "I used to work at Mount Hesse in my school holidays and then I left school to work there full-time. I always wanted to own a property like that. My love and desire to buy a property like Barunah Plains can really be traced back to my time at Mount Hesse."

Originally known as Long Water Hole, Barunah Plains was established in the 1840s and was at one point the largest sheep station in Victoria. The rambling bluestone homestead, with its wide verandahs and striking octagonal room, sits on Warrambine Creek and was built in 1866 by Scottish architects Davidson and Henderson (who built numerous grand homesteads and churches in Victoria). Surrounded by formal gardens with towering bunya-bunya pines, monkey-puzzle trees and 120-year-old elms, the property also includes bluestone stables, a coach house and a small village of outbuildings classified by the National Trust of Australia (Victoria).

From the 1850s until 1978, Barunah Plains was owned by the Russell family — pastoral pioneers who played a major role in establishing the state's wool industry and had a residence befitting their status. "Barunah Plains was on 24,280 hectares, it employed about 50 people who lived here and it was like a community — the post office was here, it had a ballroom and it was the hub of the area," Damian explains. "After World War II, the government acquired all the land for soldier settlement and in the mid-1940s Barunah was then halved in size." The property had been on the market for about six years when he bought the homestead block on 263 hectares in 2016.

"I'd looked at Barunah a couple of years prior and thought it needed a lot of work. At that point it was too big a project for me. I walked out with my head spinning and just left it. But in 2016 it was still on the market, the timing was right and I was ready for the challenge."

Damian, who is father to three daughters (Lucy, 18, Annabelle, 17, and Sophie, 14) and the executive chairman of Canny, an architectural firm and building company in Melbourne, now lives at Barunah Plains full-time. Although he has renovated numerous properties over the years, the stately homestead — with its 13 bedrooms, ballroom, formal dining room, large drawing room with a marble mantel and original grand piano ("It would be 150 years old") — has been his biggest challenge.

"Everything was rundown. We've done a stack of fencing and painting, and we've fixed a lot of things. We're at the point now where the gardens are all done and it's comfortable," the 45-year-old says.

To date, services such as plumbing and electricals have been renewed and the farm's bluestone cottage (known as Cool Cottage) and shearer's quarters, which sleeps up to 35, have been refitted as accommodation. Though it's still in operation, the property's vast T-shaped bluestone woolshed is also used for weddings and events. "We've done a huge amount of work to it: we fixed the floor, windows, roof and weatherboards," Damian says.

To continue the property's association with fine wool, Damian runs a flock of 1000 merino ewes. Whenever the girls are home (Annabelle and Sophie are at boarding school, while Lucy completed her studies last year), they pitch in with shearing or out in the paddocks. "The girls are home every second weekend and in the school holidays," Damian says. "They love to help with a bit of sheep work and enjoy getting on the motorbike to give me a hand."

For Damian, it's the ambience — the old buildings, the setting and a tangible sense of the past imbued in it all — that he loves most about Barunah Plains. And it's the satisfaction of bringing it back to the glory and grandeur of its heyday that is the best reward.

"I suppose buying this property was more about the history and architectural features than it was about the land itself," he says. "For me, the farming part is a hobby; my expertise is in recreating great houses and fixing up the infrastructure. Even so, this property has been the biggest challenge I've taken on and I've still got a long way to go — it might take another 10 years to finish. I get the biggest buzz out of it, though."

Originally published in Country Style, June 2019.

Boston ivy covers the original jackaroo quarters, which have been turned into guest bedrooms. The small structure in the foreground is an old meathouse.

A new AGA cooker in the kitchen at Barunah Plains. **FACING PAGE, CLOCKWISE, FROM TOP LEFT** Scout the Jack Russell in the woolshed; gates to the property; the old station workshop at Barunah Plains now serves as a garden shed; the dining room furniture belonged to former owners, the Russell family, and the painting is by British artist John Gray.

Lucy, Sophie and Annabelle in The Kennels paddock, so-named for its location outside the bluestone ruins of the property's old kennels.

"THE GIRLS LOVE TO HELP WITH A BIT OF SHEEP WORK AND ENJOY GETTING ON THE MOTORBIKE TO GIVE ME A HAND."

Scout perches on a guest bed. **FACING PAGE, CLOCKWISE, FROM TOP LEFT** Sheep outside the old generator room, which provided power to the station until 1960; an original basin and sink at the homestead's rear entry; Lucy in the vegetable garden; in the drawing room, Damian has added Kelly armchairs from Jardan and a silk rug from Behruz Studio.

Station horses and emus queue at a water trough on Angorichina Station in South Australia's Flinders Ranges.

Farmer Charlie Arnott and his family often picnic in Downes Paddock at Hanaminno, their property near Boorowa, NSW. **FACING PAGE** Charlie is passionate about the land.

PEOPLE

CHARLIE ARNOTT

BIODYNAMIC FARMER

BIODYNAMIC FARMER CHARLIE ARNOTT can tell you a story about every tree, gate post or paddock on his property, Hanaminno, near Boorowa on the South West Slopes of NSW. Even the property's name has a tale — his parents named it after Hāna Ranch, a working cattle property in Hawaii where they spent their honeymoon (an enterprise that coincidentally now shares Charlie's passion for regenerative farming).

Charlie grew up on Hanaminno and describes the farm as his sanctuary. Together with his wife Angelica, he now shows their children how to plant trees, muster cattle and identify birds in the undulating basalt and granite hills of the 2143-hectare property.

"I just love being in this landscape. The first seven years of childhood are about developing a relationship with nature, and that's what I endeavour to do with our children," the 46-year-old says of daughter Lilla, 9, and 18-month-old son Lordie.

A descendant of William Arnott, founder of the iconic Arnott's Biscuits Company, Charlie is maintaining the family connection to food — in his case supplying biodynamic meat to like-minded Sydney butchers such as Victor Churchill and Shiralee Organic Meats.

Charlie takes his role as a food producer seriously and shares his zest for biodynamics and regenerative farming with other landholders via regular workshops. He also produces videos on his own YouTube channel and, last year, his work was acknowledged with the prestigious Bob Hawke Landcare Award.

Each time he shifts a mob of cattle or passes through wildlife corridors of elm, honey locust and desert ash trees, Charlie pays close attention to nature's subtle touchstones, such as ground cover, diversity of grass species and soil health. "I consider myself a grass farmer and water and sunlight harvester," he explains. "We focus on what's in our control and how we use every millimetre of rain that falls."

Trees, biology and the Arnotts' Shorthorn cattle are some of the tools used to restore the landscape. Larger mobs of cattle are grazed for shorter intervals to allow the pasture to regenerate, while biodynamic soil preparations are sprayed to stimulate soil biology.

Charlie says there were a number of turning points that led him to question his relationship with the environment. After pearling in Broome and Arnhem Land, completing a Bachelor of Rural Science at the University of New England in Armidale, NSW, and a two-year stint in Sydney, he returned to Hanaminno in late 1997 to take up the reins from his father. He continued to farm using conventional methods, then in 2003 he noticed a one-day course in the *Boorowa News* called Profiting from The Drought. "I thought this will be a laugh, who profits from a drought?" he says. "I went along and it blew my mind. It showed that questioning oneself was healthy and that there were alternatives to what I was doing. I acknowledged that I didn't have a big plan for myself and the farm."

The following month Charlie attended the Resource Consulting Services (RCS) Grazing for Profit course, where paradigms were broken or challenged. He immediately stopped using chemicals and began setting goals, with a focus on "loving the grass more than the cattle. I began to think differently about the importance of people in the business, as well as how I was managing my grazing and pasture," Charlie adds.

Another turning point was meeting Angelica, an actress and former member of Australian pop group The Chantoozies. She and her two older daughters (Venus and Persia, now aged 23 and 19) were already avid supporters of organic produce, and it was Angelica's attitudes towards food and chemicals that contributed to their decision to become biodynamic farmers.

"My heritage is Sicilian Italian and food culture was everything. Dad was considered the medicine man in our family and if anyone had a malaise of any sort he would pop into the kitchen and make them something to fix it," 58-year-old Angelica recalls.

"Angelica is a wonderful cook and we always have vegetables growing. We enjoy that sense of knowing where our food comes from," Charlie adds.

These days, much of Charlie's time is spent delivering workshops on biodynamic farming and advocating for the adoption of regenerative farming. In between, he and Angelica divide their time between Hanaminno and Byron Bay, where he is involved in agricultural training and mentoring at The Farm Byron Bay.

But there's always joy in returning to Hanaminno and welcoming other like-minded people. At the end of the day, friends and family often pile in the back of the ute to enjoy a picnic in the paddock on dusk.

"I'm really positive and optimistic about regenerative agriculture; it spearheads the solutions for two main problems — the health of the planet and health of mankind. At Hanaminno we are leaving a legacy of what can be done."

Originally published in Country Style, June 2019.

CLOCKWISE, FROM TOP LEFT Charlie Arnott with his wife Angelica and their children Lilla and Lordie in front of a mob of Shorthorn breeder cattle in Clover Paddock; the breeders in Clover Paddock; Lilla skips over basalt rocks in Downes Paddock at Hanaminno.

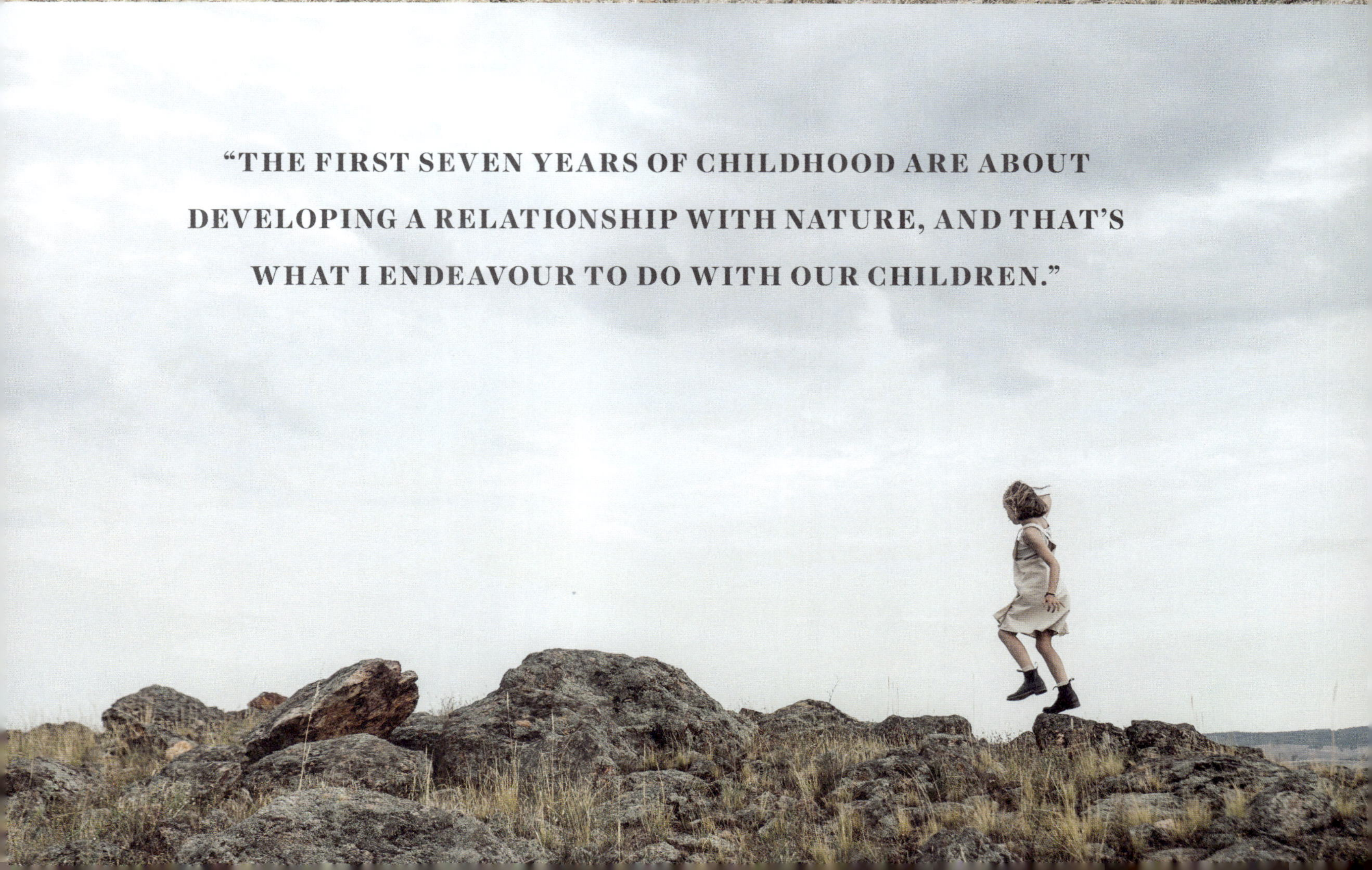

"THE FIRST SEVEN YEARS OF CHILDHOOD ARE ABOUT DEVELOPING A RELATIONSHIP WITH NATURE, AND THAT'S WHAT I ENDEAVOUR TO DO WITH OUR CHILDREN."

THIS PAGE, FROM TOP Charlie and Lilla shake out a picnic rug; the couple enjoying a wander through Hanaminno. **FACING PAGE, FROM TOP** The family at Downes Paddock. "We have many happy memories here," says Charlie; feeding the pigs.

An old church turned family home makes the perfect backdrop for Cheryl Carr's collected treasures. Local artist Hayden Roberts' *Jade* hangs above an original oil landscape painting from Aratula Traders. **FACING PAGE** A gravel path edged with bricks leads to the entrance of the converted church.

HOME

CHERYL AND MITCH CARR

BOONAH QUEENSLAND

"I LOVE THINGS THAT ARE WEATHERED AND TELL THE STORY OF WHERE THEY CAME FROM."

IN 1962, AUSTRALIAN artist Margaret Olley painted *Boonah Landscape*, daubing the rolling farmland in russet and murky greens, fringed by the craggy escarpment of Main Range National Park. Years later, when Cheryl Carr was 19 and travelling north to Cairns from her home town Taralga, in NSW, she was equally captivated by the landscape and stopped the car about 35 kilometres south of Ipswich to take a picture of a stately palm tree beside a tumbledown hut between Boonah and Roadvale.

Little did she know she was capturing the site of her future home. It wasn't until 20 years later, when she and her husband, Mitch, and their two sons moved to the country near Boonah, that she realised the palm tree in the paddock was familiar. "I wondered if it was the same one, so I asked a local," recalls Cheryl. "It was, but the hut had fallen over!"

In the years since Cheryl's first visit, she had met Mitch, an architect, and the couple had their sons, Henry, now 21, and Oliver, 19, in Queensland's Ipswich. When they looked to swap town life for the country, Cheryl rediscovered the Boonah area, the drawcard being the Bethel Lutheran church, which had been relocated to the one-hectare property. It was under contract, so she left her number with the agent and, 12 months later, it was again for sale.

"We fell in love with it — the space, the feel and the breeze," says the 46-year-old kindergarten teacher of the century-old church perched on a hill overlooking Main Range. "We'd always wanted to be out of town and this was one of the closest areas, similar to home in New South Wales, with a rural aspect."

When they moved in 2010, the eight-by-18-metre church had already been converted into a family home with a mezzanine floor and five bedrooms. The exterior was blue with burgundy and cream trim, so one of their first tasks was to enlist help to paint it in Dulux Silkwort with Dulux Domino trim, while they tackled the interior themselves, opting for a mix of cool white shades in low sheen. "In the afternoon, we get lovely sunlight coming through, so I didn't want it to be too bright," Cheryl explains.

In the living area, Cheryl had the perfect place to display the furniture she had gathered over the years. "That's the beauty of this room; it's so versatile and I wanted it to be white and calm," she says. "But I also love things that are weathered and tell the story of where they came from." As an example, the legs of an old table have been repurposed to make candlesticks and a meatsafe rescued from a shed near Glen Innes has become a place to display some of Cheryl's finds. "I had to pull it apart and straighten it up," she says.

The glass-paned hutch on the western wall is a special piece that came with Cheryl when she first moved to Queensland. "My dad was a bit of a collector; he was a farmer and I loved going with him to clearing sales," she says. "I love the thrill of unearthing things."

Before long, Cheryl decided to turn her hobby of sourcing old wares into a business and, five years ago, she listed some items on Etsy. Her brand, Albert and Grace, was named after storybook characters Mitch had conceived and illustrated a few years earlier. As interest grew, largely from stylists, so too did Cheryl's love of finding pieces and photographing them inside the church before listing them for sale. "I had bought myself a camera and it just vanished," says Mitch. "But watching Cheryl create Albert and Grace, and seeing the joy she gets from building relationships was a revelation to me. It's been lovely to see her creativity grow."

For Mitch, who spends his week travelling and commuting to Brisbane where he works as a project manager, the serenity of the church is a perfect tonic, come the weekend. "It's instantly calming," Cheryl says. "It's lovely to wake up here and be out of the hustle and bustle." Henry and Oliver love to have friends out and camp in the paddock. "It's been great for the boys growing up to have the space and it's a safe environment for young men to hang out and socialise," Mitch adds.

When friends visit, they dine under trees near the hen house where Cheryl keeps her Plymouth Rock chickens. "It's such a peaceful place with gorgeous sunsets," Mitch says. "When the sun hits the rampart of Main Range, it's just beautiful."

Originally published in Country Style, February 2018.

Looking out to the *Murraya paniculata* hedge from the front door. The 'Lucia' rattan lounge was discovered at Kmart.

Built in 1910, this house was originally a Bethel Lutheran church from Lowood, more than 60 kilometres west of Brisbane, and was relocated to the property. The weatherboards are painted in Dulux Silkwort with Dulux Domino used for the trim.

Cheryl has added her special touch to the kitchen. "I'm drawn to antique cooking utensils," she says.

CLOCKWISE, FROM TOP LEFT
Cheryl making lunch in the bright kitchen. The wall light is from Ipswich Antique Centre; Phyllis and Daphne, Cheryl's Plymouth Rock hens, outside the shed; Cheryl bought the hutch in the living area when she was only 18 — it came from a shearing shed at Taralga, NSW; the main bedroom.

Farmer Nan Bray's method of letting the sheep vary their diet has reduced the incidence of flystrike, allowing her to dispense with tail docking and the controversial practice of mulesing. **FACING PAGE** US-born Nan, who came to Tasmania in the mid-1990s, with border collie Chance.

PEOPLE

NAN BRAY

SHEPHERD ADVOCATE

NAN BRAY NUDGES the electric farm vehicle across the hilly terrain, shepherd's crook by her side and her border collie team, Janie and Chance, bounding ahead. Near the top of a ridge, she pulls up in a paddock where a flock of merinos stop grazing and heads turn in unison towards her.

Nan, an advocate of old-fashioned shepherding skills, is watching them in turn, checking their condition, the state of their wool and the pasture. On her 330-hectare property in the Tasmanian Midlands, Nan has spent years observing their grazing patterns and the choices they make from a wide range of herbs and native grasses. Her holistic approach to farm management and animal husbandry is unusual — but it appears to pay dividends.

Today Nan runs 1000 superfine Saxon merinos to produce her range of White Gum Wool yarns. She's proud to be farming ethically, and that her White Gum Wool is certified 'New Merino' for sustainability and traceability of the yarn back to the flock.

But Nan happily admits that when she bought the Oatlands property in 2000, she thought sheep were "little grass-eating animals that dogs chased". Born in Idaho, she was more familiar with cattle — there are ranchers on both sides of the family. However, as her parents had warned her not to go into farming, she took a different course, training as an oceanographer.

And then Tasmania changed her life. Nan had fallen in love with the Apple Isle during a holiday in 1995, and returned in 1996 on a year's sabbatical with a research team. By the end of it, she had applied for a position as chief of the CSIRO's Marine Division. Nan got the job and held it for six years — and by then, a new future beckoned. Science was her profession but deep down she longed to farm, and for something simpler.

"When I went for the interview for the chief's job, I bought three very high-end wool suits in San Diego," Nan recalls. "They cost an absolute bundle, but they were beautiful to wear, and I could sleep in them, then get off a plane and go straight to work. I thought with something that expensive there must be a profit in it. I was intrigued with wool — and soon I had in my head that I had to grow superfine wool."

Nan stocked the farm with sheep and cites a sick ewe named Alice and a local stockman — 87-year-old David Carnes, her farm manager for 13 years — as her mentors. Alice, now a matriarch among the flock, had suffered a difficult lambing and as Nan nursed her back to health she noticed the ewe showed distinct plant preferences. "I realised she was picking certain plants in order — chicory, plantain, lucerne, clover and then grass. She got well and I stored that knowledge away."

More knowledge was absorbed from David's lifetime of experience. "I was in the fast lane and Davey was not — he had a much kinder way with sheep," Nan says. "He empathised with them, let them move at their own pace and let the lead sheep work it out. Whereas I'd try to make things happen — and it would all go to hell in a hand basket! I learnt low-stress handling from Davey and that I was dealing with individual animals. When they choose to move, they will simply graze their way into a paddock..."

From watching Alice, Nan became convinced that when sheep can eat a wide range of plants they develop "nutritional wisdom" that allows them to balance their diets and self-medicate. She aims to have scores of plant species in her paddocks, through which the sheep graze on rotations of three to six months. She also observed that the ewes showed their lambs what to eat — but most sheep farmers are convinced of the economic benefits of early weaning. Once again David was her sounding board. "I said to Davey, 'What if we don't wean?' If I wean, I will have a bunch of babies that are clueless about how to forage. So my idea now is to leave them with their mothers so they teach their progeny how to eat."

Although she was warned that without weaning the ewes' fertility would drop, Nan has found the reverse — and this too she attributes to balanced nutrition. Her lambs also weigh more and the wool quality is up. She's currently reduced her stocking rates to ensure plant diversity but keeps one big multi-generational flock, including the old non-breeding ewes.

"It's the matriarchs who lead the flock, and show the sheep where to eat and where to shelter," Nan observes. "I'll keep them until they die."

Back in the shearing shed there is a polished floor that Nan says is great for dancing, comfortable chairs, a wood fire and a well-equipped kitchen. And, of course, the fruit of years of patient observation and hard work — bundle after bundle of soft merino yarn, which Nan has had dyed in colours inspired by the landscape.

Nan recalls the first time she set foot on Tasmanian soil, feeling immediately at home. "I was coming over the Tasman Bridge in Hobart and I saw sheep grazing in front of Government House — it was just beautiful and I said, 'Okay, this might be the place!' "

Originally published in Country Style, August 2014.

CLOCKWISE, FROM TOP LEFT
Nan with David Carnes, her retired former farm manager, and border collie Janie; Nan sends her White Gum Wool to New Zealand to be scoured and spun into yarn; the merino flock grazes on a wide variety of herbs and native plants as well as grass; the raw product — superfine merino wool.

Button grass covers the approach to the Enchanted Forest, Cradle Mountain, Tasmania.

Purchased in 2009, Matt and Andy Jackman's farm in north-west Tasmania met all their requirements for high rainfall, fertile soil and accessibility. **FACING PAGE** Matt, Harvey and Andy.

PEOPLE

ANDY AND MATT JACKMAN

DAIRY FARMERS

"THE HERD NOW NUMBERS MORE THAN 400, AND THEIR DEEP RED COATS STAND OUT AGAINST THE BRIGHT GREEN HILLS..."

IN THE STAFFROOM at Red Cow Dairies, an A4 notice in bold type outlines what's important for this family-owned business in Oldina, north-west Tasmania. Among the bullet points are 'sustainable', 'ethical' and 'environmental' but the line that stands out the most is a question: 'How big do you want to get?'

Andy Jackman and her husband, Matt, started dairy farming in northern Victoria in 2001 and decided to move to Tasmania in 2009 to escape the severe drought. On the Bass Strait boat trip they brought with them their son Harvey, now five, and 370 Aussie Reds, a leading breed of dairy cows developed for Australian conditions. "It was easier than shifting furniture, that's for sure," Andy says. "And cheaper!"

The drought was so drastic that the family found the 155-hectare property (through 'desktop research') and moved in the space of six weeks. "Everyone tried to dissuade us from coming here," Andy says. "They told us, 'You don't want to go to Oldina; it's way out in the backblocks...' We actually had to convince the agent to take us to view the property."

Matt and Andy were looking for a farm that was near a small community and not too far from an airport; they still have a property in Victoria's Appin South that needs regular attention. Other prerequisites included a high rainfall, fertile soil — and a reasonable asking price.

"In a perfect world, you'd probably have less hills because that does take its toll on the animal," Andy says. "And in terms of a farm-gate location, you'd be right on the Bass Highway. But at the time we weren't looking for a cheese-manufacturing location."

The herd now numbers more than 400, and their deep red coats stand out against the bright green hills where Matt and Andy have chosen to farm using low-intensity techniques and non-conventional fertilisers. They knew they needed to do more than merely milk cows to make their family business work and decided to venture into cheesemaking, which Andy learnt while completing a diploma of food science and technology at the National Centre for Dairy Education in Werribee, Victoria.

When she first moved to Tasmania, Andy did a year-long marketing course which, among other things, introduced her to the importance of branding and colour. "I remember the designer talking about McDonald's and Coca-Cola, and I thought, 'I'm going to do either red or yellow.' "

And so, in April 2012, Red Cow Dairies, with its distinctive bright red artwork, was born — it's the only artisan cheese manufacturer in the country to use the milk of Aussie Reds. The red packaging is a vibrant contrast to the creamy white of the triple cream brie, mozzarella, camembert, washed rind, Persian-style fetta and cream cheese.

The couple recently decided to stop producing non-homogenised full-cream milk for retail sale. "It's awesome milk and our customers love it, but it's high volume and low return," Andy says. "So we've decided to develop the cheese instead. You need to pick your niche."

Moving out of the milk business also means Harvey's parents will be less flat out. "It's intense and a full-on lifestyle choice — we do everything, from growing and mowing the grass to milking the cows," Andy says. "We turn our cheeses individually and look at them and ask, 'Is this one ripe enough for packaging?' It's that level of intensity that we pride ourselves on, and you can't do that when you're trying to do everything else to please everybody."

With this sort of resolute focus, the Jackmans should have little trouble deciding how big they want to get.

Originally published in Country Style, March 2014.

CLOCKWISE, FROM TOP LEFT Matt and Harvey out in the paddock; the herd now numbers more than 400; the Aussie Reds were brought from the mainland when the Jackmans moved to Tasmania in 2009; maturing camembert: each cheese is checked daily.

"WE DO EVERYTHING FROM GROWING AND MOWING THE GRASS TO MILKING THE COWS."

Developed in the 1980s, the Aussie Red combines well-known red breeds, such as Ayrshires, Illawarras or Holsteins, with Scandinavian sires. **FACING PAGE** Heading back to the milking shed.

With grandparents just up the hill, this family farm in the Byron Bay hinterland is an idyllic home for Edward Rawlings and Jeanie Wylie and their young children. **FACING PAGE** Edward Rawlings with his daughter, Evelyn.

HOME

JEANIE WYLIE AND EDWARD RAWLINGS

NASHUA NSW

BEING ABLE TO watch their children head off across the paddock, with their 10-month-old heeler-cross Rosie running alongside, is one of the reasons Edward Rawlings and Jeanie Wylie are farming their verdant 48-hectare property in subtropical Nashua, NSW.

That the children — Frederick, seven, Evelyn, four, and two-year-old Arthur — can make a detour up the hill to their grandparents' place in time for morning tea is an added bonus. Andy and Sandra, Edward's parents, are partners in the Byron Bay hinterland property and divide their time between the farm and Brisbane, around two hours' drive north, where their other children, daughters Emma and Polly, live with their families.

"It's like having fairies at the bottom of my garden," says Sandra. "The only rule is that the children need to let Mum or Dad know they're coming up. They drop in unannounced so we'll have cheese and biscuits and talk about their week. They feel very at home here."

"It's a bit of an old-fashioned idea," says Edward of the arrangement. "But it works for everyone."

In 2011, after years living and working in Sri Lanka and England, Edward, 40, and Jeanie, 38, decided they wanted to return to Australia and raise a family in the countryside. Initially, they lived with Sandra and Andy at Edward's childhood home, a small farm in Deebing Creek, near Ipswich, Queensland.

Edward and Jeanie treated the move as a trial run to test their ideas around sustainability and growing food and to see if they enjoyed farming life. The couple spent four years in Ipswich and discovered that they loved it, and over time the idea of moving to a larger property grew — as did the notion of doing it all together.

Sandra and Andy had bought their Ipswich property when they married in the late 1970s but five decades on, the city had arrived on their doorstep. "When we moved there, we lived on a dirt road and were surrounded by paddocks but by the time we left, it had been consumed by housing," says Sandra. "Andy wanted a rural bolthole, but not the responsibility of running a farm. Jeanie and Edward are making this possible. We're just lucky we can share."

In the two years since the extended family made the move to Nashua, their mission has been to get everyone housed. Thrift, and a desire to reuse and repurpose, were behind their decision to bring as many structures and materials from Deebing Creek as possible. It took months — and 10 removal trucks filled with their possessions. Four additional wide-load trucks carried sections of the original family home, a tin farm shed, and a small cottage that was once the Ipswich coach house and has now become their farmstay, The Cottage.

It was Andy and Edward's idea to relocate the buildings. Deebing Creek had been sold to a developer and the structures on it were about to be demolished. "It felt so much better to repurpose them," says Edward. "It's all been so useful," adds Andy, "and we've used everything we brought."

When they arrived, there were two existing buildings on the property — a farmhouse, which Jeanie and Edward are in the process of renovating, and a cottage, the original farm manager's home, where Sandra and Andy live. The cottage had a small, square floorplan with a traditional layout with small rooms, an enclosed verandah and a bathroom at the back.

With the help of architect Chris Hills, who had also built the original house in Deebing Creek, and interior designer Mary Durack, both based in Brisbane, the cottage is colourful, warm and cosy. Encouraged by Mary, Sandra brought a lot of her furniture from Ipswich to the new house. "She understands that you can make old things look good again, and that it's all about memories," says Sandra.

"So much of the new house is exactly as it was because we brought almost everything with us. The kitchen, the bedrooms, even the bathroom. The only thing that's different is the view."

Meanwhile, Edward and Jeanie's place is a work in progress as they've sunk all their energy into building a viable farm business. A verandah linking the children's bedroom wing to the main house has been built. But paint schemes and floor sanding will have to wait.

For now, Edward and Jeanie's plan is to grow food and open the farm to visitors through their new venture Frida's Field. "We want to bring people onto the farm and create a place where the community can come together to eat," says Jeanie.

The building blocks have fallen into place with a herd of Angus Wagyu cross cattle, the start of a large market garden with rabbit-proof fencing, and lots of citrus and stone-fruit trees, including limes, oranges, peaches and plums.

"It's Edward and Jeanie's deal," says Andy. "But we've been working on it together and it's been lots of fun."

Originally published in Country Style, December 2018.

Pots from Scotland Yard Antiques in Marburg, Queensland, and a rug from Ishka on the verandah of Edward and Jeanie's house.

CLOCKWISE, FROM LEFT A chest of drawers housing Sandy's napery; Jeanie and Edward's farmhouse; Santa Barbara bistro chairs from Naturally Cane in The Cottage farmstay; Sandra (left) and Andy love spending time with their family: Arthur, Frederick, Jeanie, Edward and Evelyn. **FACING PAGE** Evelyn and Frederick Rawlings with their blue and red heeler cross Rosie.

"ANDY WANTED A RURAL BOLTHOLE, BUT NOT THE RESPONSIBILITY OF RUNNING A FARM. JEANIE AND EDWARD ARE MAKING THIS POSSIBLE. WE'RE JUST LUCKY WE CAN SHARE."

The family's onsite farmstay, known as The Cottage, is available to book online and is a private world unto itself. It faces away from the other buildings so guests can enjoy total seclusion and privacy.

The bedroom of The Cottage has a lampshade in Candid Moment Gardenia fabric from Fabric Traders and Belgian flax bed linen from West Elm. **FACING PAGE, CLOCKWISE, FROM TOP LEFT** The Cottage is painted in Dulux Teahouse; the bed canopy in Sandra and Andy's bedroom was made by Hans Welding Works in Ipswich and designed by Mary Durack, while the bedspread was bought during travels in Mumbai; Evelyn with Rosie, their blue and red heeler cross, enjoying the wide open space on the farm; the sink and taps are from Restoration Station in Brisbane and the curtain is made of fabric from Fabric Traders.

Norm moves a wool bale in the woolshed. **FACING PAGE** Glenwood's sheep are SRS (soft rolling skin) merinos.

PEOPLE

PIP AND NORM SMITH

WOOL PRODUCERS

PIP SMITH ALWAYS dreamt that she and her husband of 20 years, Norm, would one day create beautiful garments straight off their sheep's backs.

"I thought, 'Wouldn't it be great to tell our story through a product made exclusively from our wool?'" says Pip, as she stands with her childhood sweetheart, overlooking Glenwood, the 2800-hectare property near Wellington, in central NSW, where the Smith family has a long history. Pip and Norm's five children are the fifth generation of Smiths to live at Glenwood. "They don't know how lucky they are really," says Norm, "but one day they will understand." Today, the family shares the property with various dogs, cats and 10,000 merino sheep.

There are compelling reasons for Pip to tell their story. For years, it upset her that the high-grade wool Norm produces on Glenwood, ethically and sustainably with so much love, ended up mixed with inferior wool at auction.

"We'd watch the buyers for international fashion houses come around, and they'd say, 'The Glenwood wool is the best so I'll take 50 bales.' Then they'd go and mix it with 50 bales of cheaper wool, and that just seemed so wrong after all the work and study Norm has done to breed such beautiful merinos. That's where the idea of making a garment with every wool fibre traceable back to Glenwood came from. I just didn't get around to acting on it for so long because the kids were so little."

Today, Chloe, 19, Amber, 18, twins Will and Maggie, 16, and Daisy, nine, are more self-sufficient, so last year Pip, who grew up on a property just over the hill, decided the time was right.

Ably abetted by Norm's brother Ian, a former trade commissioner, and Sydney designers Manuela Strano and Tess Lloyd, she started Love Merino. It sells limited-edition scarves made from the finest single-source merino wool, traceable back to a Glenwood mob of sheep. Some of the hand-printed and dip-dyed designs are inspired by the native clovers and grasses found on Glenwood. Other designs pay homage to Norm's mother and grandmother, who cultivated the gardens around the homestead during the decades of family history here.

Love Merino's Sydney launch in October 2016 literally stopped traffic. "We took two of our sheep and walked them down the main street of Balmain, which seemed to create a lot of interest," says Norm, winner of the NSW 2011 Farmer of the Year award.

Love Merino has a growing customer base in Australia, America and Europe, and is also attracting attention from global fashion brands such as Muji, Patagonia and Van Heusen. All of which have made the five-hour drive from Sydney to see the holistic land and soil management and animal husbandry the Smiths implemented when they took over from Norm's late father, Brian, in 1996.

Interest, says Norm, is driven by increasing consumer demand for ethically sourced fabrics. Glenwood sheep are paddock-fed, and in the early 2000s the Smiths stopped the controversial practice of mulesing. Instead, they looked to the work of former CSIRO researcher and veterinarian Jim Watts to breed an SRS (soft rolling skin) merino, which doesn't have as many skin folds as a traditional merino and is less likely to attract blowfly.

"In Australia, only about three per cent of merino farmers are doing what we are doing, and I believe as an industry we are losing market share because we have a reputation for mulesing in this country," says Norm. "Big retail players such as GAP, Marks and Spencer, and Country Road are looking to take their business to New Zealand or South America because consumers are increasingly aware of animal rights issues, and are demanding that their fabrics are ethically sourced."

Every eight months, a team of shearers arrives at Glenwood to spend 12 days removing 200 bales of wool from the Smiths' flock. Each bale holds 200 kilograms. Forty bales go to long-time supporter, Forbes manufacturer Warwick Rolfe of Woolerina. Like all Australian wool, it is then processed offshore into yarn.

On its return, the Smiths purchase it back from Rolfe, and have it made into fabric. They have recently been approached by some of Australia's largest retail stores, including David Jones, to stock Love Merino but for now Pip is happy to sell online. In the future she would like to start a designing and dispatching outlet from nearby Wellington.

"For me, Love Merino is the culmination of a long-time dream to share the story of our gorgeous wool with others," says Pip.

"For a long time, I've known that my husband, Norm Smith, is one of the most exceptional men in the Australian wool industry, but I finally feel that Love Merino might help to bring him the recognition I believe he deserves."

Originally published in Country Style, February 2017.

"FOR ME, LOVE MERINO IS THE CULMINATION OF A LONG-TIME DREAM."

Norm, Pip, Daisy and Amber.

CLOCKWISE, FROM TOP LEFT The Love Merino range includes 'pashminos', throws and baby blankets; the Glenwood sheep graze in large mobs to mimic nature; it takes a team of four shearers 12 days to shear Glenwood's flock of 10,000 merinos; their wool is fine, soft and lustrous. **FACING PAGE** Pip and Norm Smith met at high school before marrying in 1996. "I've always felt Norm and I marrying was written in the stars," says Pip.

WORDS Heather Nette King
PHOTOGRAPHY Sharyn Cairns
STYLING Heather Nette King

WORDS Virginia Imhoff
PHOTOGRAPHY Marnie Hawson
STYLING Lee Blaylock

WORDS Virginia Imhoff
PHOTOGRAPHY Lisa Cohen
STYLING Tess Newman-Morris

WORDS Virginia Imhoff
PHOTOGRAPHY Lisa Cohen

WORDS Claire Mactaggart
PHOTOGRAPHY Mark Roper

WORDS Catherine McCormack
PHOTOGRAPHY Mark Roper

WORDS Virginia Imhoff
PHOTOGRAPHY Lisa Cohen
STYLING Tess Newman-Morris

WORDS Tracey Platt
PHOTOGRAPHY Mark Roper
STYLING Nicola Sevitt

WORDS Hilary Burden
PHOTOGRAPHY Sharyn Cairns
STYLING Charlotte Bell

CREDITS

WORDS Virginia Imhoff
PHOTOGRAPHY Marnie Hawson

WORDS Freya Herring
PHOTOGRAPHY Mark Roper

WORDS Claire Mactaggart
PHOTOGRAPHY Marnie Hawson, Jared Fowler
PHOTOGRAPHY ASSISTANT Nicola Sevitt

WORDS Skye Manson
PHOTOGRAPHY Lisa Cohen
STYLING Beck Simon

WORDS Andrew McUtchen
PHOTOGRAPHY Sharyn Cairns
STYLING Glen Proebstel

WORDS Skye Manson
PHOTOGRAPHY Lisa Cohen
STYLING Beck Simon

WORDS Virginia Imhoff
PHOTOGRAPHY Mark Roper
STYLING Leesa O'Reilly

WORDS Gretel Sneath
PHOTOGRAPHY Sharyn Cairns

WORDS Virginia Imhoff
PHOTOGRAPHY Mark Roper

CREDITS

WORDS Samantha Van Egmond
PHOTOGRAPHY Marnie Hawson
STYLING Hannah Brady

WORDS Virginia Imhoff
PHOTOGRAPHY Marnie Hawson
STYLING Lynda Gardener and Belle Hemming

WORDS Virginia Imhoff
PHOTOGRAPHY Michael Wee

WORDS Claire Mactaggart
PHOTOGRAPHY Michael Wee

WORDS Claire Mactaggart
PHOTOGRAPHY Abbie Melle

WORDS Hilary Burden
PHOTOGRAPHY Sharyn Cairns

WORDS Barbara Sweeney
PHOTOGRAPHY Abbie Melle

WORDS Claire Mactaggart
PHOTOGRAPHY Marnie Hawson
PHOTOGRAPHY ASSISTANT Nicola Sevitt

WORDS Barbara Sweeney
PHOTOGRAPHY Marnie Hawson
STYLING Nicola Sevitt

WORDS Alex Speed
PHOTOGRAPHY Mark Roper

COVER PHOTOGRAPHY
Sharyn Cairns

BACK COVER PHOTOGRAPHY
Kara Rosenlund
Wild brumbies in Mount Kosciuszko National Park, NSW.

SCENIC PHOTOGRAPHY CREDITS
Front endpapers Jared Fowler
Kata Tjuta, also known as The Olgas, Central Australia, Northern Territory.
John Laurie
p2, 98-99 Sharyn Cairns
p84-85, 130-131 Jared Fowler
p38-39 Mark Roper
p224 Prue Ruscoe
p4-5, 6-7, 14-15, 64-65, 112-113, 150-151, 174-175, 196-197 Michael Wee
Back endpaper Michael Wee
Grazing cattle in South Burnett, Queensland.

COUNTRY STYLE

EDITOR Kylie Imeson
DEPUTY EDITOR Hannah James
CREATIVE DIRECTOR Sarah Farago
ART DIRECTOR Bernhard Schmitz
ART DIRECTION & DESIGN Chi Lam
CHIEF SUB-EDITOR Sue Ramsey
COLOUR CORRECTION AND RETOUCHING Matus Kundrat
PRODUCTION Kara Stead

are media *books*

ARE MEDIA
CHIEF EXECUTIVE OFFICER Jane Huxley

ARE MEDIA BOOKS
GENERAL MANAGER – LIFESTYLE & FOOD Nicole Byers
DIRECTOR OF BOOKS David Scotto
Printed in China by Leo Paper Products Ltd

International Rights Enquiries
internationalrights@aremedia.com.au

Published in 2023 by COUNTRY STYLE
Are Media Books are published by
Are Media Pty Limited
54 Park St, Sydney; GPO Box 4088,
Sydney, NSW, 1028 Australia
phone (+61) 2 9282 8000
aremediabooks.com.au

A catalogue record for this book is available from the National Library of Australia.
ISBN 978-1-92569-586-1 (hardback)

To order books, phone 136 116 (within Australia)
or order online at magshop.com.au

ACKNOWLEDGEMENT OF COUNTRY
Are Media acknowledges the Traditional Owners of Country throughout Australia. We pay our respects to Elders past and present.

Albert & Grace etsy.com/shop/AlbertandGrace
Cathy Penton Atelier cathypentonatelier.bigcartel.com
Charlie Arnott charliearnott.com.au
B&B Flowers Instagram.com/b_n_b_flowers
Blue Ginger Fine Foods & Café bluegingerfinefoods.com
Bruny Island Cheese Co brunyislandcheese.com.au
Bush Roses bushroses.com.au
Frida's Field fridasfield.com
Harvest Moon harvestmoon.com.au
Heatherly Design heatherlydesign.com.au
Limewash Vintage facebook.com/limewashvintage
Little Red Barn littleredbarn.com.au
Leeuwin Grass-Fed Beef leeuwingrassfedbeef.com.au
Love Merino lovemerino.com.au
Merimbula Gourmet Oysters merimbulagourmetoysters.com.au
Philip Wolfhagen philipwolfhagen.com
Red Cow Dairies redcoworganics.com.au
Rundell & Rundell rundellandrundell.com.au
Shene Estate & Distillery shene.com.au
Two Rivers tworiversgreentea.com.au
White Gum Wool whitegumwool.com.au
Woodstock Resources woodstockresources.com.au

Summer comes to a wild stretch of coast near Western Australia's Margaret River.